JEWISH CULTURE IN EASTERN EUROPE
The Classical Period

BOOKS BY
MOSES A. SHULVASS

Die Juden in Wuerzburg Waehrend des Mittelalters 1934

Rome and Jerusalem (Hebrew) 1944

Chapters from the Life of Samuel David Luzzatto (Hebrew) 1951

The Jews in the World of the Renaissance (Hebrew Version) 1955

In the Grip of Centuries (Hebrew) 1960

Between the Rhine and the Bosporus 1964

From East to West 1971

The Jews in the World of the Renaissance (English Version) 1973

JEWISH CULTURE IN EASTERN EUROPE

The Classical Period

BY

MOSES A. SHULVASS

KTAV PUBLISHING HOUSE, INC.
New York
1975

Library of Congress Cataloging in Publication Data

Shulvass, Moses Avigdor, 1909-
  Jewish culture in Eastern Europe.

  1. Jewish learning and scholarship—Europe, Eastern.
2. Jews in Eastern Europe—Intellectual life. I. Title.
DS113.S48   943.8'004'924   74-34140
ISBN 0-87068-273-3

Manufactured in the United States of America

CONTENTS

PREFACE

When the Science of Judaism came into being early in the nineteenth century, it paid little attention to the vast masses of East European Jewry, their past and their culture. The heroic stand of Franco-German Jewry in the crucible of the Crusades and the grandeur of the Golden Age in Spain captured all the attention and talent of the early generations of modern Jewish scholars. Only late in the nineteenth century did Russian Jewish intellectuals begin systematically to uncover and describe the historical destiny and cultural achievements of their own community, which, numerically, was the largest aggregate of Jews in our entire past. Their promising work, alas, was cut short when the First World War came to an end. The same holds true of the equally promising and energetic beginnings of Jewish scholarship in Poland during the period 1919-39.

Thus, now, late in the twentieth century, the story of the East European Jewish past and its culture is still largely unwritten. The dynamic life of the East European Jew, his aspirations throughout the ages, and his own typically East European Jewish culture beckon to be explored and described. During the millennium of its existence, Polish Jewry experienced several heydays, the residual heritage of which is still a source of enchantment to our own generation, which witnessed in horror the transformation of Polish Jewry from living community to legend. It is therefore up to our generation to continue from the point at which the work of Jewish scholars in Russia and Poland abruptly ended, so that the Jewish experience in Eastern Europe shall become an open book.

The present study proposes to describe one chapter of that experience: the cultural tensions of East European Jewry, and the creativity that resulted from them during its classical period, i.e., from its inception to the first decades of the seventeenth century, when the Old Polish Commonwealth took a decisive turn toward disintegration.

This book was written with the help of a research grant from the Memorial Foundation for Jewish Culture. The Decalogue Society of Lawyers in Chicago and the Alumni Association of Spertus College of Judaica assisted in its publication.

My colleague David Graubart read the manuscript. My daughter Phyllis Gelman and my colleague Byron L. Sherwin made many felicitous linguistic suggestions. My friend David G. Singer prepared the index. Mrs. Mildred Crane, of the Spertus College of Judaica secretarial staff, prepared the typescript.

My sincere thanks are due to them all. But first and foremost my profound gratitude is due to my wife, Celia. Her assistance was manifold and constant.

Spertus College of Judaica   Moses A. Shulvass
December, 1974.

CHAPTER ONE

THE HISTORICAL BACKDROP

I.

The earliest Jewish communities in Eastern Europe existed in the Crimea and on the northern shores of the Black Sea. In the first century C.E., only a few years after the destruction of Jerusalem, Jews already lived in various colonies originally established by Greeks in this region. The available information tells of a Jewish settlement which lived peacefully and enjoyed a degree of organized religious and communal life. The sources indicate that during the early Middle Ages Jews also lived in what is known today as the Southern Ukraine.

This Jewish settlement began to expand when the king and part of the Khazar people, who had established a strong state in those regions, converted to Judaism or, perhaps, Karaism during the eighth century. The persecutions of the Jews in the neighboring Byzantine Empire induced some Jews to emigrate to the friendly, partly Jewish, Khazaria. Likewise, some Jews arrived in Khazaria from the teeming Jewish centers in Western Asia, from over the Caucasus Mountains, and through the Gate of Nations. A legend relates that the Jews even tried to convert Duke Vladimir of Kiev (980–1015). Vladimir did not become a Jew; instead he introduced Christianity into Russia. The Jewish settlement in the Ukraine grew nevertheless, and it is likely that when the Khazarian kingdom was destroyed a number of the Jewish Khazarians were absorbed within Ukrainian Jewry. The Jewish community in the capital city of Kiev sustained a relatively high level of culture and attained a degree of importance. It seems that Southern Ukraine's Jewish population, together with the remnants of the Jewish Khazarians, were obliterated by the terrible invasions of the Tartars during the first half of the thirteenth century. In the decades following the Tartar invasions no Jewish settlements are known to have existed in the Ukraine.

Russia's oldest Jewish community was the result of immigration from Byzantium and the Near East. But, as all signs indicate, the Jewish settlement of Poland emerged as a result of the immigration of Jews from Germany. The incredible slaughter of Jews in Western Europe preparatory to the first Crusade (1096), apparently initiated the significant historical process which transferred great numbers of Jews from Germany to Poland within several hundred years and bestowed a specific Western character upon the Jewish people in Eastern Europe.

II.

The history of the Jewish community in Eastern Europe is henceforth closely related to the destiny of Poland. The kingdom of Poland appeared about the year 1000. At the beginning it was a weak kingdom that still had to overcome the painful process of having been fragmented for a long time into a mosaic of small principalities. In 1241 a considerable part of the country was totally devastated by a Tartar invasion. Gradually, the country strengthened itself and became an important factor in Eastern Europe. During the second part of the thirteenth century many immigrants arrived from Germany and from other parts of Western Europe to settle the desolate land, build cities, and develop commerce. At the same time, the state began to expand in a southeasterly direction. Before the end of the fourteenth century, the most significant event in Polish history occurred—Poland's unification with the principality of Lithuania. Through this union Poland acquired a considerable part of the Baltic Sea Coast and a vast territory in the Ukraine. Poland was now a great power and its influence reached "from sea to sea"—from the Baltic in the North to the Black Sea in the South. In the realm of international trade, Poland's significance also grew rapidly. In Western Europe great markets for Polish agricultural products opened. A golden epoch began in the history of the Polish state which lasted until the end of the sixteenth century.

The developments just described prepared the ground for the large-scale immigration of Jews from Germany. In their German homeland, the Jews had been experiencing political, social, and economic degradation. The Crusades, the anti-Jewish legislation of both the State and the Church, and the repeated blood accusations, followed by bloody pogroms, convinced the Jews more and more that there was no future for them in Germany. They began to call that country, in which they had lived for more than a thousand years, the "Land of Calamity" (*eretz gezerah*). Not only did the number of Jews who escaped the country grow rapidly, but the leaders of the Jewish community urged their co-religionists to leave the land soaked with Jewish blood.

The Jewish refugees from Germany escaped in different directions. Some of them went to Southern France and from there to Spain. Larger groups settled in Italy and in the Balkan peninsula. But the simplest alternative was Poland. Recently devastated by the Tartars, Poland needed immigrants. The still backward Polish economy of the thirteenth century offered the many experienced merchants and money lenders among the Jewish immigrants from Germany considerable opportunity. In addition, the Polish kings and princes received them in a friendly manner. The government's interest in founding new cities also helped to create favorable conditions for the immigration of urbanized Jews. In addition, the language was familiar. The Polish cities of the thirteenth century, overflowing with immigrants from Germany, were, in fact, German settlements where German remained the spoken language for a long time.

Small wonder that considerable numbers of German Jews, in search of a new home, moved eastward into Poland. It is probable that shortly after the First Crusade small groups of

Jews from Germany and from Bohemia reached Poland. However, the earliest documentary evidence about Jews in Poland dates from the end of the twelfth century. Quite naturally the first Jewish settlements in Poland appeared in the western provinces, close to the German border. In the fourteenth century, however, we find Jews and Jewish communities scattered all over the country.

The rapid expansion of the Jews in their new homeland was to a great extent the result of the friendly attitude of the rulers toward Jewish immigrants. In 1264 Duke Boleslaw of Kalisz granted them a charter which became the legal foundation for their settlement. This charter, modeled after a constitution granted the Jews a few decades earlier in Austria and in Bohemia, was quite favorable to them. It became the *Magna Charta* of medieval Polish Jewry.

Of utmost importance for the development of the Jewish community in Poland was the fact that when a great wave of Jewish immigrants from Germany arrived, refugees from the terrible persecutions during the Black Death, Poland was ruled by King Casimir the Great (1333–1370). In 1334 he granted the charter obtained by the Jews of the Duchy of Kalisz in 1264, to all the Jews of his kingdom. He later granted them other favors. The historian Jan Dlugosz, who wrote his *History of Poland* about one hundred years later, relates that the great king fell in love with the Jewess Esterka, the daughter of a tailor from a small town. In this fashion later generations tried to explain the remarkable friendship of the great king for his Jewish subjects.

The Jewish community of Poland continued to grow after Casimir's death. When Lithuania united with Poland in 1386, several Jewish communities existed in her Ukrainian regions. It is difficult to determine whether these were remnants of the Jews of Southern Ukraine and of Khazaria who had survived the Tartar invasions; or whether they were German Jews who had penetrated that far eastward. During the fifteenth century new immigrants arrived from Germany in large numbers. A series of local expulsions sent whole Jewish communities from

Germany into Poland including their rabbis and other communal functionaries. When at the turn of the century the Jews were expelled from Spain, a certain number of them also came to Poland. As a result of all these migrations, the number of Jewish communities in fifteenth-century Poland was six times as large as it had been one hundred years earlier. The first Jewish presence in Warsaw dates from 1421. In 1430 the city had a Jewish Street. Obviously, the number of Jews was rapidly growing. At that time the Jews did not reside solely in the large cities where the Gentiles also spoke German. They were now scattered in many cities and towns, and it is estimated that they numbered thirty thousand.

III.

The Jews from Germany who settled in Poland entered various fields of economic endeavor. Many of them had had considerable experience in the field of banking and money exchange. We find Jews who became farmers of state mints during the thirteenth century. In the fourteenth and fifteenth centuries money lending became a source of income to a considerable number of Jews. However, during the second part of this period money lending began to lose ground among them. Trade, local as well as international, began to attract them more and more. A certain number of them, in Poland as well as in Lithuania, earned their livelihood in the various branches of agriculture. It is also worth noting that there were a number of Jewish physicians, some of them immigrants from Spain.

During the fifteenth century we find fairly well organized Jewish communal institutions all over Poland. The high level of communal organization in this young settlement should, of course, be attributed to the fact that the immigrants brought with them old, solid forms of communal life. The most important aspect of the communal organization was the fact that within the framework of medieval society, the *Kehillah* was a religious as well as an administrative body whose duty it was to care for the safety and welfare of the "Jewish street." It also wielded considerable judicial power. Within this communal framework an important process began to take shape. Many small communities located in suburbs or villages, which had been under the control of the neighboring large Kehillahs, began to establish themselves as independent communal organizations.

IV.

The rapid growth of the Jewish population, its penetration into all provinces of the country, and its influence in economic life evoked considerable resentment among the clergy and the burgesses. The clergy looked askance at the friendly attitude of the State toward the Jews; the burgesses saw in them, typical city dwellers as they were, dangerous competitors in the economic struggle.

By the middle of the fourteenth century, when the clergy became aware of the remarkable friendship of Casimir the Great toward the Jews, they began to incite the populace against them. This anti-Jewish propaganda resulted in a number of riotous outbreaks against the Jews. The outbreaks of this type even increased in number during the fifteenth century. In 1399 the first trial took place in Poland in which a Jew was accused of stealing and defiling the holy wafer—an accusation which was quite common in Western Europe. The Polish clergy's campaign against the Jews was characterized by methods similar to those practiced in Western Europe. However, the outbreaks against the Jews in Poland were not nearly so dreadful as those in Western Europe. In their plight the Jews found help among the magnates and the lesser gentry, who derived many profits from the Jews. In addition, many of the nobility were well-educated men, zealous advocates of the ideals of the Renaissance and humanism. They were by far the most liberal part of the Polish population. As already mentioned, the burgesses were on the side of the clergy. They conducted an energetic as well as a systematic fight against the commerce of the Jews, and often succeeded in curtailing the right of the Jews to do business. The immediate result was that Jews began to abandon commerce and became craftsmen and artisans. These occupations later became a major factor in the economic life of the Jews.

Not being content with partial success in their fight against the Jews, the burgesses began to demand their expulsion. When news of the many local expulsions in Germany reached Poland, it whetted the appetite of the burgesses to act likewise. In 1453 the famous preacher John Capistrano visited Poland and "became frightened" when he saw the large number of Jews living in the capital city of Cracow. He, therefore, vigorously preached against them and demanded that they be expelled. This demand erupted again in 1492 under the impact of the expulsion of the Jews from Spain. Increased propaganda of the Polish anti-Semites then caused a new wave of pogroms. In a number of cities the burgesses' dream was fulfilled and the Jews were expelled. The king even granted a number of cities the dubious privilege of *de non tolerandis Judeis,* the right not to tolerate Jews within their limits. In 1495 Duke Alexander of Lithuania, who later ascended the Polish throne, expelled all the Jews from his territory. He hoped that the confiscation of their property would fill his empty coffers. He quickly realized, however, that the expulsion of the Jews was a mistake; they were recalled and their communal property was returned to them.

In spite of all their troubles, the partial expulsions, and the eternal struggle for the right to earn a living, the Jews found Poland and Lithuania a paradise in comparison with Germany. Consequently, Jews from Germany continued coming. When in the sixteenth century Poland became one of the most powerful and prosperous countries in Europe, its Jewish settlement, too, became the leading Jewish community. The Golden Age of Poland became also a Golden Age for the Jewish people in Eastern Europe, who surpassed other Jewish communities in economic and cultural importance.

V.

The political rise of the Polish commonwealth persisted throughout the sixteenth century. The union with Lithuania immensely increased its territory. The vast areas of the South Ukraine, which lay waste for hundreds of years following the Tartar invasions, now began to be colonized. Poland's export was increasing; the richest countries in Western Europe, England and Holland, and the Scandinavian countries in the North, bought the products of its agriculture and forestry. Humanism and Reformation evoked a mighty response and vigorously stimulated all cultural endeavors.

No wonder Poland was still attractive to Jews of other lands. New Jewish immigrants from Germany arrived, and they continued to come all through the sixteenth century and in the first part of the seventeenth, when unmistakable signs began to indicate that Poland, together with its Jewish community, was entering an era of economic and political decline. During the sixteenth century many Jews also arrived from Bohemia. Their number in Cracow became so large that they were even able to establish a communal organization of their own, recognized by the authorities. Some came to settle in Poland even from Italy, where the Jews lived fairly peacefully during the Renaissance.

As a result of all these great migratory currents, and thanks to the economic prosperity of the country, Poland's Jewish community immensely increased in size. It has been estimated that about the year 1550 the Jewish community of Poland numbered between 70,000 and 100,000, second only to its sister community in Turkey. One hundred years later, on the eve of the "Great Catastrophe," the Polish Jewish community numbered between 300,000 and 500,000, the largest territorial concentration of Jews in the world. About one quarter of them lived in the territory of the Duchy of Lithuania.

The main occupation of the Jews during the sixteenth century was still all forms of commerce. This was especially true of the western and central provinces of the commonwealth.

However, the number of Jewish craftsmen was constantly increasing. In the then newly colonized areas of the Ukraine, the main occupation of the Jews was the farming of tolls and taxes and leasing of estates. They became a well-to-do class. Most of the Jewish sections in the cities had beautiful stone houses; wealthy men built beautiful synagogues, often designed by famous architects. The Jewish sections in many cities and towns expanded considerably in area, and a network of specifically Jewish settlements sprang up outside the cities which refused to admit them.

The growth of the Jewish population, its economic success, and the influence which Jewish magnates exerted in the royal court, provoked, as had happened two hundred years before, a bitter attack from the clergy and other anti-Semitic circles. The struggle of the Catholic clergy against the various Protestant groups was accompanied by an intensification of the fight against the Jewish "heretics." And when the Counter-Reformation achieved a decisive victory over the Protestants, it was followed by a deterioration of the position of the Jews. The anti-Semites now began to fight the Jews with literary means. The country was virtually flooded with anti-Jewish pamphlets, satires, and caricatures. Special books were written to discredit the Jewish physicians in the eyes of the Christian population. The number of the blood libel trials was on the increase, especially during the first part of the seventeenth century. At the same time the accusations against Jews for allegedly defiling the holy wafer also increased. More and more cities won the privilege *de non tolerandis Judeis*. Ironically, the Jews, too, obtained similar privileges, the right *de non tolerandis Christianis*. The Jewish sections of various cities and all the Jewish communities of Lithuania had the right not to admit Christians, because they were overcrowded. Despite all this, the Jew generally lived in fairly friendly relations with his Christian neighbor, with whom he traded and for whom he worked as a craftsman. It is worth noting that in the Lithuanian provinces of the commonwealth, where the burgesses were fewer and weaker as a group, anti-Semitic riots were much rarer and the familiar tension between Jew and Gentile was less intensive.

The growing anti-Semitism was the direct cause of two major developments among the Jews of Poland around the turn of the century. Ever-growing numbers of Jews began to leave the big cities and to settle on the private territories of the magnates. At the same time many began to leave the western provinces of the commonwealth altogether and to migrate southeast to the areas of the new colonization in the Ukraine. As a result of these movements many villages and towns sprang up, totally inhabited by Jews. The magnates received the Jews in a friendly fashion, similar to that manifested by the kings of Poland a quarter of a millennium earlier. The Jews greatly contributed to the economic development of the vast waste areas controlled by the noble families; they introduced trade and commerce and brought wealth into the land. In 1539 the king formally gave up his jurisdiction over the Jews living on the territories of the noblemen. This change in the legal status of a considerable part of the Jewish population contained a great potential danger. These Jews to a large extent now lost the protection of the central government and were exposed to the whims of individuals.

The second process which Polish Jewry experienced also had broad dimensions; namely, the migration of great masses from the western provinces eastward and southward. Jews who became tired of the enmity of the populace in the cities of the West, or victims of the economic attack of the burgesses, as well as individuals in conflict with the communal leadership, began streaming into the Ukraine. The Ukraine was a frontier country, and the Jews who settled there were true pioneers who brought material and spiritual culture with them. Economic opportunity was virtually unlimited. Constituting the most civilized part of the population of this wild and waste land, they cooperated closely with the Polish landlords, who developed the country, and were an important factor in the tremendous effort to colonize it. Their main occupation was in the area of management. They were the leading farmers of customs and other categories of taxation; they rented distilleries, breweries, inns, and similar enterprises. And as the opportunities were great, the wave of Jews going to the Ukraine persisted uninterrupted till the year of the Great Catastrophe (1648). Jews even came directly to the Ukraine from Germany and Italy. During the second part of the sixteenth century, many new communities were formed. In the immediate neighborhood of Kiev and Bratslav, there were as many as fifty densely populated Jewish towns.

The only troubling aspect of the Jewish developments in the Ukraine was the one-sidedness of the Jewish occupations. As managers and lessees of enterprises owned either by the Polish government or by Polish noblemen, they were considered oppressors by the Ukrainian, Greek-Orthodox peasant population, or at least the representatives of the Polish Roman-Catholic oppressors. The hatred shown the Polish noblemen in the Ukraine and their Jewish agents on social, religious, and ethnic grounds steadily grew, so that in 1648 when the great revolt erupted, led by Bohdan Chmielnicki, it brought with it a terrible calamity to the Jewish population of the Ukraine and of the Polish commonwealth at large.

VI.

With the growth of the Jewish population and the expansion of its economic endeavors, its communal organization, the *Kehillah,* increased in importance. This was an epoch of great cultural aspirations and the *Kehillah* was called upon to satisfy these needs. The growing tension between Jews and Gentiles imposed additional responsibilities upon it. The activities of the *Kehillah* were, therefore, steadily expanding and becoming more and more ramified. Besides the official *Kehillah,* an impressive number of voluntary societies sprang up to care for the various religious, social, and cultural needs. Special communal trustees, *gabbaim,* were appointed to ransom Jewish captives and to collect alms for the needy in the Holy Land. Various communal officials cared for the sanitation of the Jewish streets and supervised prices, weights, and measures.

The ban or excommunication was a mighty and often cruel instrument at the disposal of the *Kehillah* to impose its control. The court of the *Kehillah* even had the authority to sentence Jewish criminals to punishment. The importance of the *Kehillah* manifested itself in the title given to its head in official documents: Burgomaster of the Jewish Community. The *Kehillah* was usually controlled by a handful of wealthy aristocratic families. Their dictatorial rule caused great damage to the Jewish masses more than once. Already in the sixteenth century attempts at revolt against the rule of the aristocrats were made. It seems that the major complaints were directed against the *Kehillah's* misuse of its right to impose the *herem* ban. In the middle of the seventeenth century, therefore, some limitations upon this right were enacted.

A major development in the communal organization of the Jews was the establishment of the Council of the Four Provinces. The idea of a central Jewish communal organization was born simultaneously among the Jewish leaders and in government circles. The Polish Treasury believed that a national *Kehillah* would simplify the collection of taxes from the Jews. In those times the Treasury did not have a well-organized tax-collecting machine at its disposal. It therefore resorted to the system of imposing the various taxes in lump sums on different social and professional groups. It was then the duty of the groups to collect the taxes from their members and deliver the lump sums to the Treasury. Each local *Kehillah* thus had to serve as collector of taxes for the government. With the spectacular increase in the number of the Jewish communities throughout the commonwealth and their spread over vast areas, it became increasingly difficult for the Treasury to negotiate separately with each local *Kehillah*. Consequently, the government became inclined to force the Jewish communities of the various provinces to unite on a regional basis.

Simultaneously the idea of establishing a central communal organization gained popularity within the Jewish community as well. The struggle against the growing anti-Semitism among the burgesses and the clergy became more involved. To deal with such tragic phenomena as blood accusations was far beyond the capabilities of small local *Kehillahs*. The necessity for enacting important economic legislation also called for centralized communal organs.

The first step towards a central organization of Polish Jewry was the establishment of *Vaadim Geliliim,* Regional Councils, in various provinces of the commonwealth during the first decades of the sixteenth century. The next step was the creation of a central rabbinic court. Many Jewish merchants from all over the country met regularly at the fairs in Lublin and Jaroslav, and because of their business transactions the need for a Jewish Fair-Court became evident. With the establishment of this court the first truly central organ of Polish Jewry became a fact. In 1581 the Treasury decided to change the system of collecting taxes from the Jews. From then on, more and more often one lump sum was imposed annually on all the Jews of the commonwealth. The task of justly partitioning this sum among hundreds of communities and of collecting their contributions was a major effort, and the establishment of the *Vaad Arba Aratzoth,* the Council of the Four Provinces, that is to say, of the four provinces of Jewish settlement in Poland became inevitable. To be sure, the primary task of the Council was to serve as a tax agent of the Treasury. However, from the very first moment of its inception the Council began to consider and take effective action on all great Jewish religious and communal issues. It met twice annually, in Lublin and in Jaroslav, during the great Fairs held there. Consequently, the already established Jewish Fair-Court automatically turned into a sort of Jewish Supreme Court with seven leading rabbis as justices. The institution served as a Court of Appeals in relation to the local *Kehillah* courts and as a mediator in litigations between *Kehillahs,* Jewish regional councils, and other Jewish public agencies. The Council elected a permanent executive committee to implement its decisions and to act in emergency situations between sessions.

The Lithuanian Council was the most important of all the regional councils. It enjoyed autonomous status and held joint sessions with the Council of the Four Provinces to discuss issues affecting the Jews in both parts of the commonwealth. The importance of the central organ of Polish Jewry was considerable, and official documents termed it the *Parliament of the Jews of Poland.*

The growth of the Jewish community in the Polish-Lithuanian commonwealth from a tiny group of settlements to the largest Jewish community in the Middle Ages, is one of the great processes in the history of the Jewish people. It was accompanied by an equally important process of growth and development in the religious and cultural spheres.

CHAPTER TWO

CULTURAL BEGINNINGS

We find the oldest traces of Jewish spiritual life in Eastern Europe during the eleventh century in Kiev and its environs. Old Russian chronicles note that the Jews of those regions conducted missionary activities amongst the Russian population and that these activities met with opposition from the Church. The names of the missionaries who attempted to spread the Jewish faith in Russia are not known. No doubt, they were learned Jews who were well versed in the religious literature of the Jewish people and knew how to interpret it to Gentiles.

The first Jewish scholar named by the sources is the twelfth-century rabbi Moses of Kiev. He was a great scholar who corresponded with learned Jews in the Near East and Western Europe. He exchanged scholarly letters with the famous head of the rabbinic school in Baghdad (Iraq), Samuel ben Ali. We also find Rabbi Moses visiting France and residing in the school of Rabbenu Tam, who was the greatest Jewish scholar in Western Europe, and a great and vigorous communal leader of French Jewry. We cannot ascertain when he visited France. Nor do we know whether he ever returned to his home in the Ukraine. If he did return, Moses of Kiev imported a new method of studying Jewish law and lore to his native country: the way of the *Tosaphists,* of whom Rabbenu Tam was one of the first and certainly one of the greatest. This new way employed a dialectic method of study which stimulated the scholarly initiative of the students. Besides Rabbi Moses, other Jewish scholars from Kiev came to Western Europe. Some of them went as far as England and Spain. The city of Kiev was not the only place that could boast of Jewish scholars. Vladimir and Chelm, located farther west, had some men versed in Jewish law.

The intellectual interest of the Jews of the Ukraine, as we have seen, drew its nourishment both from the Near East and Western Europe. Furthermore, it was enriched by a stream of books imported from Babylonia (Iraq), which at that time was a major center of Jewish learning. Various sources tell about the availability in the Ukraine of Jewish books from Babylonia. There was obviously a demand for them.

Not much, however, survived from the literature of the Ukrainian Jews of those times. If any books were written there, they were lost in the Tartar invasion of the thirteenth century. But some traces remained of a "commentary produced in Russia," probably a commentary on the Talmud or some of its parts.

Less spectacular, it seems, was the spiritual life of the Jews in Poland during the twelfth and thirteenth centuries. A scholar from Bohemia who visited Poland in about 1200, related that most of the Jewish communities in Poland lacked learned men. The scarcity of spiritual leaders was so serious that the communities were often compelled to entrust the combined duties of cantor, rabbi, and teacher to one man. These men rarely possessed all the necessary qualifications for the threefold job. Under such circumstances there developed a friendly atmosphere for visiting scholars. Besides the Bohemian scholar, some other learned Jews who had visited Poland by the end of the twelfth and the beginning of the thirteenth century reported warmly in Western Europe on the new, growing Jewish settlement in Eastern Europe and its spiritual aspirations.

Little is known of the spiritual life of the Jews in Eastern Europe during the fourteenth and the first part of the fifteenth century. Quite often a blackout is spread over the Jewish past in a certain area or during a certain epoch. Such "silent centuries," however, frequently were times of transition to very great epochs. So it was in Eastern Europe.

About the year 1400 a very learned immigrant from Prague settled in the capital city of Cracow. This immigrant, Yomtov

Lippmann Muehlhausen, was a very colorful personality. His profound knowledge was coupled with deep insight into the religious and philosophical literature of medieval Jewry. In addition, he mastered Latin, was versed in the New Testament and the writings of the Church Fathers. Not much is known of Lippmann's origin. He resided in various cities in Germany, and it is likely that in Erfurt he headed a yeshivah. Most of his life he lived in Prague, the capital of Bohemia. As a medieval Jew, during his lifetime he faced many dangerous situations, but always managed to escape unharmed.

Being learned in Jewish as well as in Christian lore, Lippmann was often involved in religious disputations with Christians, laymen as well as clergymen. Some of these were mere friendly debates. Others, however, and especially one with a Jew who converted to Christianity, were forced upon the Jews. In all these skirmishes Lippmann seems to have been quite successful. He obviously knew how to refute the arguments of his opponents with wisdom and wit.

After a long career of representing his people in religious controversies in Germany and in Bohemia, Lippmann settled in Cracow, at that time a point of attraction for many Jewish immigrants from Bohemia. Little is known of his activities in his new home. According to a contemporary, he wrote there his famous work, *Sefer hanitzahon, The Book of Victory,* which is a guide to the defense of the Jewish religion in disputations with Christians. Generally, such discussions dealt with the interpretation of certain passages in the Bible. Lippmann, accordingly, arranged his book in the form of a commentary on those crucial passages of Holy Writ. The book is composed of 354 paragraphs, the number of days in the lunar year. Medieval authors often used such symbols in their works. Each paragraph discusses a different passage of the Bible. Interpretations by Christians and by Jewish sectarians, as well as Lippmann's refutations, are presented with clarity and simplicity, so that even laymen could understand and use them. The author's unusual debating skill is evident in the humorous and often sarcastic manner in which he discusses his themes. A striking number of bold, almost "modern" thoughts reveal a man who was already breathing the air of the nascent humanism. Though Lippmann's work was first printed in 1644, it was very popular in the more than two hundred years before its publication, as the unusually large number of handwritten copies preserved in many libraries indicates. Lippmann is also the author of other books in various literary areas.

Although little else is known about Lippmann's activities in Cracow, it is hard to imagine that a scholar and leader of his stature lived in the capital city in complete retirement. We should rather assume that Lippmann strongly influenced the rising Jewish community, and regard him as one of the men who prepared the ground for Cracow's later fame in the area of Jewish learning. But a hundred years had to pass before the city became the great spiritual center of East European Jewry.

Warsaw, Poland's capital of later times was still a small provincial town. It had, however, its Jewish community, from which some "literary" traces have survived. Notes in Hebrew found in old documents show that in these early times, the thirties of the fifteenth century, Jews in Warsaw mastered the holy tongue. Such information is always indicative of some degree of Jewish culture.

To be sure, learning was not yet universal among Polish Jews. A German scholar, Israel, a rabbi in Bruenn (Moravia) who could closely observe what was happening in Poland, tells that among the Jews of Cracow no scholars could be found. The situation was somewhat different in Posen. Our informant tells of an immigrant rabbi who served the Posen community without remuneration. The rabbi was evidently a wealthy man, and he spent considerable amounts of money to foster Torah learning in his new home. Somewhat later we find in Posen another immigrant rabbi from Germany, Moses Minz. He was a jurist of high standing and very active in communal affairs in his homeland. His advice and decision in matters of religion were sought even from distant places. When he settled in Posen in 1474, he was about forty years old. It seems that he remained in Posen till the end of his life. Similar was the situation in Lemberg, the leading community in southeastern Poland, where in the latter part of the century a yeshivah with a large number of students was functioning. Its head was an otherwise unknown scholar, Rabbi Levi Kikiness, who died in 1503. Immigrant rabbis from Germany lived in a number of other cities, as well. A sprinkling of Sephardic rabbis from Spain and Portugal also found their way to Poland. To attract additional rabbis and scholars, Polish Jewry began to exempt them from paying taxes. In those times Jews paid all their taxes to the local *kehillahs,* and those, in turn, satisfied the government by paying lump sums for the Jewish community as a whole. When, therefore, a rabbi was exempted from paying his tax to the Jewish community, he was, in fact, exempted from paying taxes altogether.

The main center of Torah learning in East Europe during the second part of the fifteenth century, however, was again Kiev, the capital of the Ukraine. Not much is known about the spiritual life of Kiev's Jews during the preceding one hundred and fifty years. A note in an old, handwritten prayer book tells that in 1310 a number of rabbis arrived in Kiev from the Near East. After a "silent" century and a half we find in the Ukraine a blossoming Jewish settlement about which the famous prophecy, "For out of Zion shall go forth the law, and the word of the Lord from Jerusalem" (Isaiah 2:3; Micah 4:2), could be paraphrased to read, "For out of Kiev shall go forth the law and the word of the Lord from Starodub" (a town to the north of Kiev). A scholar from the Crimea stated in a letter written in 1481, that in Kiev "many pursue studies and seek knowledge." Jewish scholars lived also in Russian cities located farther to the north. The movement of "judaizing" among the Russian clergy and the emergence of the *Subbotniki,* Sabbath observers, which made a deep impact on contemporary Russian society, was not without inspiration from Jewish scholars. It is likely that some writings of Kievan Jewish authors found their way to the *Subbotniki.*

The most eminent scholar was again a man named Moses and known as the "Exile from Kiev." He was born into a rabbinic family in 1448. We do not know where he was born; but we do know that as an adolescent he went to Constantinople, then a great center of learning, to study Torah and the sciences. After only a few years he was an accomplished scholar in Hebrew philology, Bible, and Talmud. He was equally expert in the secret lore of the Kabbalah. Of the sciences, astronomy appealed to him most.

In 1470, at the age of twenty-two, Moses, like his father, became rabbi of Kiev. For twelve years he lived peacefully, studying and teaching. Then disaster struck. In 1482 the Tartars attacked the city. Among their many captives, to be sold on the slave markets of the Near East, were the rabbi's children. The invaders also seized his valuable library. As many did in similar situations, the rabbi travelled from one Jewish community to the other to collect the necessary money. Jewish communities usually responded generously whenever the ransom of captives was involved.

In Lutsk and Troki, during his peregrinations in Lithuania, Rabbi Moses became acquainted with Karaite scholars. With these representatives of the Jewish sect, which, while accepting the Bible rejected the Talmud, the learned wanderer had heated debates. The disputations gained widespread fame; they were heard of even in far-off Constantinople, where Moses was still well remembered as a brilliant young rabbinical student.

After a long journey, Moses now had the necessary funds to redeem his children. The family was finally reunited in Kiev. The rabbi, however, could only live peacefully for a few short years. In 1495 Alexander, Grand Duke of Lithuania, ordered the expulsion of all Jews from his territories. Since Kiev was under Alexander's control, its Jewish community had to seek a new home in the Crimea. It was this expulsion which later prompted the rabbi to call himself "Moses the Exile." Moses settled in the city of Kaffa, where, as the spiritual leader of the Jewish community, he was very influential for many years. When Grand Duke Alexander revoked his order of expulsion in 1503 and permitted the exiles to return to their homes, Moses of Kiev did not avail himself of the opportunity. Evidently tired of his many wanderings, he remained in Kaffa, where he died in about 1520.

Among the books authored by Moses the Exile there is a grammar of the Hebrew language, a treatise on the Jewish calendar, commentaries on the Pentateuch and on the Book of Ecclesiastes, and several kabbalistic discourses. Of all his works only the kabbalistic book *Shoshan Sodoth, The Mystic Rose* has been published. This work, written during the years of his wandering, greatly consoled him during those turbulent times. A part of his captured library was discovered in the nineteenth century.

CHAPTER THREE

THE FORMATIVE PERIOD

Torah learning in Poland became firmly established in the beginning of the sixteenth century. Within only a few decades that country became the leading center of Jewish learning. All the great developments had their origin in Cracow. As we have seen, only some fifty years earlier, a great German rabbi had deplored Cracow's lack of Jewish scholars. At the turn of the century, a radical change occurred. Another learned immigrant settled in Cracow and he succeeded, more than Moses Minz in Posen or Yomtov Lippmann Muehlhausen a century earlier in Cracow, in leading Torah learning to great heights.

Jacob Pollack, known as the *Baal Hahilukkim,* "The Master of Analysis," was probably born in Germany in about 1460. Some scholars suggest the name Pollack to indicate that he was a native of Poland. Jacob himself tells only that he was a descendant of Rashi, the great scholar who lived in France during the eleventh century.

When young Jacob Pollack was a student of Talmudic lore, we find him in Bavaria. He probably studied in Nuremberg, in the yeshivah of Jacob Margalith, one of Germany's foremost Talmudic scholars. Pollack's fame as a great scholar began to spread early. He first held a rabbinic position in Prague. From there he came to Poland where he married the daughter of the wealthy banker Moses Fischel, himself an immigrant. Being a member of an influential family that had close relations with the royal court helped him to obtain the position of the rabbi of Cracow. He was appointed to this office in 1503 by a royal decree.

While there is no doubt that his wife's family was influential

22

in securing for Jacob Pollack the rabbinate of the capital city, this was not the sole factor involved. For he was a scholar of rare quality with strong inclinations to communal leadership. The patent of King Alexander of June 21, 1503, stated it clearly: "As the Jew Jacob Pollack is dear to us because of his diligence and familiarity with the Torah of Moses and her laws, we command herewith to appoint him and raise him to the position of a rabbi of the Jews. We also grant him the authority to arbitrate conflicts between Jews in accordance with the law, to eliminate litigation, to correct what is wrong, to improve the virtues of the people, and to carry out in accordance with our will . . . various other tasks that are connected with the position of a rabbi according to the Torah. We therefore command the Jews . . . to recognize the Jew Jacob Pollack as a rabbi according to your Torah, and to obey him in all matters pertaining to his position."

Jacob Pollack was the first rabbi in Poland to be appointed by royal decree. From the document quoted above it is difficult to determine whether Jacob was made chief rabbi of the capital city of Cracow, of the region of Cracow, or perhaps even of all Poland. A folk tradition explains his name Pollack as an acrostic of the Hebrew words *Prag waagafeha, Lublin, Kraka,* meaning, "Prague and its surroundings, Lublin and Cracow." If this tradition is correct, Jacob Pollack exercised rabbinic authority over two provinces with a dense Jewish population: Southwestern Poland and Lublin and its vicinity.

Jacob's qualities as a great scholar and a forceful, though somewhat impulsive personality, no doubt impressed the king and many others very deeply. In those Renaissance times everybody held these qualities in high esteem. Many years later Moses Isserles, himself a rabbi in Cracow, echoes his initial impression of Jacob's greatness by calling him *hazaken,* "the Elder," an honorific title usually reserved only for great scholars. By the title "the Elder" Isserles probably wanted to indicate the pioneering character of Pollack's rabbinic activities. He thought that a certain religious custom should remain in force solely because it was introduced by him.

In this light Moses Isserles understood Jacob Pollack after the latter's death. Jacob's contemporaries, however, could not easily accept the passionate temper and belligerency manifested by the great scholar, a child of the Renaissance with all its advantages and faults.

We often find the great rabbi entangled in all kinds of conflicts, such as a dispute with colleagues on a complicated case in the field of Jewish marriage law, or in a personal quarrel with his opponents. Once, the rabbi's enemies succeeded in bringing him to trial, and minstrels sang a satirical song about him (*ein Spoettlich Lied*). Finally, the passionate rabbi started a lonely fight against all the leading rabbis of his time, was excommunicated, and compelled to leave Cracow. After several years of wandering in various countries, Jacob Pollack returned to his home but does not seem to have regained his rabbinic position. Finally, he left Cracow again and headed for the Holy Land. In a letter in which he recommended a certain book to the public, he signed his name "Jacob Pollack of Jerusalem." This indicates that he reached the Holy Land and probably spent his last years there. A chronicle written shortly after his time tells us that he died about 1530.

The stormy life of Jacob Pollack did not prevent him from becoming the legitimate pioneer of Torah learning in Poland. As soon as he arrived in Cracow he founded a yeshivah. This school by far surpassed in importance the yeshivah established earlier in the century in Lemberg. The great personality of its founder, the new method of study introduced by him (see below), and certainly also the financial means of the Fischel family, which were at his disposal, attracted many students. While Germany had formerly been the center of higher Jewish studies for aspiring young men, Cracow now replaced it. Students in the hundreds, including some from Germany, studied at Jacob Pollack's school. A brilliant product of this school was Rabbi Shalom Shakhna, the founder of the second leading Polish academy, the yeshivah of Lublin.

Old traditions, reaching back to Jacob Pollack's contemporaries, insist that he was the creator of a new method of re-

search in the Talmud, known as *Hilluk,* analysis, or *Pilpul,* pep-
per, a fanciful name indicating the sharpness of the intellectual
power required to employ it. Modern research had not yet
arrived at a final conclusion concerning the origin of the Pilpul
method. It is certain that Jacob Pollack was called *Baal Ha-
hillukim,* meaning the analyst, the pilpulist. Later scholars
stressed the fact that either he himself created this method or
at least introduced it into the yeshivahs of Poland and let it
to triumph. Some scholars believe that Pollack's Pilpul is the
same as that which was practiced in several yeshivahs in
Bavaria and known as "Nuernberger" and "Regensburger"
because it was developed in Nuremberg (where Jacob Pollack
himself studied) and in Regensburg. Others think that there is
a new element in Jacob Pollack's Pilpul. He employed the
Pilpul method in such an extreme manner, they reason, that
the old, established yeshivahs of Germany did not want to accept it. He, therefore, decided to go to Poland, the country with
new Jewish opportunities, in order to introduce his method
into its yeshivahs, still in their infancy.

It seems impossible to arrive at a final conclusion, because
Jacob Pollack left hardly any literary works. But precisely
this, and especially the reason why he abstained from the
literary fixation of his teachings, tells us very much. He did
not write any works, we are told, because he was concerned
lest his pupils should accept them uncritically and abandon
their independent research in the Talmud. For Jacob Pollack,
whose literary abilities were considerable, this was a great
sacrifice. A still extant legal opinion, written by him against
a decision of an Italian rabbi, reveals its author not only as an
alert and aggressive fighter, but also as a writer with a beautiful
style who knew how to use the Hebrew language effectively.
Jacob Pollack's greatest desire, however, was to train his students to think independently. To achieve this goal he decided
to promote the *Pilpul,* or *Hilluk,* as the main method of study.

Modern attempts to describe the Pilpul's characteristics have
not been very successful. As most scholars have a negative
attitude towards it, their descriptions stress its negative aspects.

Some of them like to compare the Pilpul to the sophistic and casuistic methods employed by certain groups of Greek pseudo-philosophers. They term Jacob Pollack's method *bilbul,* confusion, rather than *pilpul,* analysis. Others describe it as "thought gymnastics devoid of a positive task." Certain scholars, however, who in their youth studied in yeshivahs and knew the method of Pilpul from experience, found it comparable to certain forms of modern jurisprudence. The central task of the Pilpul—writes a renowned and original Talmudic scholar—is to extract from two related thoughts a common basic concept and then to go on to develop it logically and systematically.

To be sure, the method of Pilpul and the term itself were known many centuries before they became popular in the Bavarian yeshivahs. The Talmud reports that some scholars conducted their learned debates in such an ardent manner that they are to be compared to fighters on the battlefield and merited being called *baaley terisin,* that is to say, shield bearers. A scholar who manifested extraordinary debating ability was called in the Talmud *baal pilpul,* a master of Pilpul. Similarly, student discussions of legal problems were termed *pilpul hatalmidim,* the students' Pilpul. From time to time the teachers in schools where the Talmud came into being purposely provoked discussions based upon illusory reasoning in order to train their students in the art of debating. Also in their lectures the sages intentionally employed an exaggerated, artificial language, full of comparisons, metaphors, and riddles in order to impress the students and induce them to study. From time to time they even overdid it. In the academy of Nahardeah in Babylonia they accused the sister academy at nearby Pumbeditha of employing exaggerated Pilpul exercises, comparable to "drawing an elephant through the eye of a needle" (Baba Metsia 38b). Nevertheless, one of the leading scholars of the Talmud held that "none is to be given a seat on the Sanhedrin unless he is able to prove the cleanness of a reptile from biblical texts" (Sanhedrin 17 a), although the Bible clearly declares reptiles to be ritually unclean.

The necessity of employing the Pilpul as a method of study

in the yeshivah, despite its inherent pitfalls, results from the fact that the Talmud, by its nature, lends itself to research and analysis rather than casual reading. When one studies the Talmud on a yeshivah level he cannot be satisfied with simply translating its Aramaic text into the vernacular. One cannot even be satisfied with interpreting the text. He has to analyze it. Thus, continuously confronted with the need to analyze and compare passages from various Talmudic tractates, the student often finds himself compelled to resort to the Pilpul method. In fact, the yeshivah student has the right, and is even expected to dispute or challenge the teacher's interpretation and offer in its place his own opinion. A class in Talmud is, therefore, for all practical purposes, a discussion group rather than a note-taking student body. As soon as a contradiction or an inconsistency is noticed, the *kushia,* the questioning argument, is applied as a potent lever of criticism. And since certain types of contradictions are quite frequent in the collectively written Talmud, some yeshivahs developed their own methods of resolving them, which became known by the name of the yeshivah of their origin. In this fashion, the above-mentioned types of Pilpul, known as *Nurenberger* and *Regensburger* were developed. The method of Pilpul was well known and employed among the Christian Schoolmen of the Middle Ages. They, too, trained their pupils in close reasoning and in the art of making fine distinctions.

A close observation of the different types of Pilpul and a perusal of various Pilpul manuals reveals that the method is based on two actions: comparison and analysis. By means of comparison common elements are discovered in concepts which seemingly are alien one to the other. Similarly, the analysis aims at proving that contradictions existing between different concepts are only illusory, and that these actually have very much in common. Both these means of reasoning usually bring the sharp-minded thinker to his goal, much as the mathematician is able to reach his goal in different ways. In order to stimulate discussion, the yeshivah teacher would select as the theme of his lecture a passage of the Talmud which reports a *pelugta,* a controversy, between two Talmudic sages. During the lecture one of the students would arise as a *makshan,* an inquirer, and present the teacher with a *kushia,* a questioning argument, directed against the opinion of one of the *baale pelugta,* the parties to the controversy. It would seem that in this way the inquirer would identify himself with the other *bar pelugta,* the Tanna or Amora holding the opposite opinion. Very soon, however, the inquirer would proceed to question the opinion of the other *bar pelugta,* Tanna or Amora, with whom he previously seemingly identified himself. As a result of such a critical approach to all opinions expressed in a Talmudic controversy, all concepts would gradually become clarified and the students would understand all the various reasons which caused the different *baale pelugta,* the parties to the controversy, to arrive at their opinions.

In order to be able to participate in a class that studied by the method of Pilpul, a student had to acquire a vast erudition and at the same time train himself in the art of debating. Soon sharpmindedness became more important than erudition since the student always had to be ready and alert to pose questioning arguments, to detect contradictions, and to reconcile them. The Pilpul method was also employed in Rabbinic literature. When discussing the daily religious practices, rabbinic authors would use simple and uncomplicated reasoning. But the same scholars, when they wrote novellae on the Talmud, that is, theoretical treatises on legal discussions recorded therein, would embark upon long, complicated, and subtle pilpulistic analyses.

There is no doubt that as long as use of the Pilpul was controlled, it served as a mighty lever to develop the abilities of many students and to make them self-reliant in their encounter with the "sea of the Talmud." Pilpul trained them to compare concept with concept and to derive from definite laws decisions in ambiguous cases. In addition, these contests of the mind were, to many young people, a favored sport, because they added excitement to the study of legal problems, often dull by nature. Here one could relax the reigns of his fantasy. "Thinking became full of vigor, charged with passion" (Heschel).

Chronological considerations lost all significance. It was legitimate to discuss differences of opinions between scholars who lived hundreds of years apart and to consider them a direct "controversy." "If disagreement was discovered between a view held by Rabbi Akiba Eiger of Posen, who lived in the nineteenth century, and Rabbi Isaac Alfasi of Morocco, who lived in the eleventh century, a Warsaw scholar of the twentieth century would intervene to prove the consistency in the learning carried on throughout the ages" (Heschel). The scholar permitted himself to do just that because he deeply believed that the Talmud and the vast literature which grew up around it possessed an imminent logic of its own which transcended time and space. Hence the Pilpul attracted many students. It also evoked some interest in the Gentile world. Several Christian scholars described it, and a certain Leonhard Appoltus even was granted a Doctorate of Philosophy in 1737 for a dissertation, not too successful, which dealt with the manifold varieties of the Pilpul.

Nevertheless, the Pilpul has always been a controversial method viewed with distrust by many great scholars. To some of them it was in total disrepute. We shall have an opportunity to discuss this problem in later chapters. At this point it should suffice to say that the main reason for the emphatic challenge of certain scholars to the Pilpul method is because it is often difficult, if not altogether impossible, for the learner to disengage himself from it after it is no longer useful. That the Pilpul is often constructed on illusory foundations is best illustrated by a story which attempts to demonstrate the greatness of Jacob Pollack's mind. His students, we are told, once tore a few pages from his Talmud. Their teacher succeeded, nevertheless, in bridging the gap satisfactorily, as if the text before him had not been mutilated.

In this, probably apocryphal, story, Jacob Pollack's admirers desired to describe his unusual ability to apply the Pilpul method. They also clearly revealed that their idolized way of study could indeed become dangerous. Scholars, captivated by the Pilpul method, used to entangle artificially a number of quite different legal problems. Then, like magicians, they would untwine the knot with one pull. The Pilpul also sometimes negatively affected important works of Rabbinic literature. More than once a great Rabbinic author would abandon his main theme in order to construct an "elegant" Pilpul. The strongest argument advanced against the Pilpul, however, is that its task was not to attain the truth, but rather to defeat the opponent. The exaggerated Pilpul does not contribute to the clarification of the problem under discussion; it aims only at the stupefaction of the opponent. It does not address itself to the opponent's thinking power; it only attempts to silence him. For all these reasons the Pilpul became a bone of contention in the Jewish scholarly world from the time when Jacob Pollack firmly established this new method of study in Poland.

The introduction of the Pilpul exerted a far-reaching influence on the entire field of Torah learning in Eastern Europe. To begin with, the tendency towards pilpulistic studies brought about a certain "division" of the Talmud. Some of its tractates became a preferred subject in the yeshivahs because their texts easily lent themselves to pilpulistic discussions. Other tractates, whose texts are more "neutral," came to be studied superficially and with less enthusiasm. The Pilpul also affected that branch of Rabbinic literature where it was least expected—the area of homiletics. By its nature, a homiletical discourse belongs to a literary genre that addresses itself to the heart, while the Pilpul belongs entirely to the realm of the mind. Nevertheless, even the homiletical discourse was conquered by the Pilpul on its victorious march. Similarly, the traditional pre-holiday sermons that the rabbis delivered on the Great Sabbath and on the Sabbath of Repentance, the task of which was to teach the people the laws of Passover and of the Feast of Tabernacles, became pilpulistic excursions in which the rabbis manifested their skill in the area of Talmudic jurisprudence instead of instructing the people. The Pilpul also deeply influenced the literature of Jewish mysticism, the Kabbalah. When the Kabbalah began to spread in Poland early in the seventeenth century, local authors began to produce kabbalistic works with a definite pilpulistic flavor. During the heyday of the Pilpul several handbooks were written as guides for the proper use of its different types.

The great success that the Pilpul enjoyed in Poland is probably to be attributed to the vigor with which the forceful Jacob Pollack promoted it. Its chances were also enhanced by the easier availability of Hebrew books which flowed from the newly established printing presses of Cracow and Lublin. And it was also to a great degree the cheerful and dynamic disposition of the Polish Jew which made him responsive to a method of study such as the Pilpul. Against this backdrop Rabbi Shalom Shakhna, the first native Talmudic scholar, could now firmly establish his teacher's way of learning among the growing numbers of students of the Talmud.

Rabbi Shalom Shakhna was born into an aristocratic family. His grandfather, after whom he was named, and his father Yosko, were among the most prominent financial agents of the Polish kings. Yosko soon became the wealthiest Jewish magnate in the country. Most of his financial enterprises were concentrated in the vicinity of Lublin. He lived in the city during the latter part of his life, the only Jew permitted to dwell outside the ghetto.

When Yosko died in 1507 he was survived by his widow and a few small children. The widow, Golda, was a "woman of valor" in every respect. Yosko willed her all of his real estate and his other enterprises. He also entrusted the education of his children to her. Golda survived her husband a full quarter of a century. She managed to preserve the family's fortune and even expanded her business activities. She also provided her sons, Pesah and Shalom Shakhna, with the opportunity to study Torah. In time, Pesah became the manager of the family's economic interests. Shakhna, too, was active in the area of high finance, and performed some services for the king. His main interest, however, was in the area of learning. He went to Cracow to study under Jacob Pollack, and for some time he attended a yeshivah in Posen. He was very successful in his studies and became the first native Polish-Jewish scholar of high stature.

Contemporaries agree that Rabbi Shakhna was a very learned man. Even an official document of the king of Poland stresses his unusual erudition (*non vulgarem scienciam*). Official documents term him *Doctor Judeorum Lublinensium*, which shows that he was the official rabbi of Lublin's Jewish community. In December, 1541, the Polish government appointed him to a much higher post. He became regional rabbi of Little Poland, so that henceforth he had authority over the religious life of Jews in the vast territory of Southern Poland. He was authorized to confirm appointments of rabbis to the local communities. Only those who received his recognition were entitled to perform marriages or grant divorces. The power he wielded was so great that he even sentenced Jewish criminals to bodily punishments. About ten years later, when the Polish government decided to abolish the office of regional rabbis, Shalom Shakhna still retained the authority of rabbi of the Jews of Lublin and of its entire province (*wojewodztwo*).

Lublin was a place where much-frequented fairs were regularly held. Top leaders of the Jewish communities, who were among the richest merchants in the country, attended these fairs. They often used their business meetings for the purpose of discussing problems of interest to the Jewish public. From these informal fair gatherings grew the "parliament" of the Jews of Poland, the Council of the Four Provinces and its Central Court. These communal bodies did not fully develop until several decades after Shakhna's death. There are, however, indications that Rabbi Shakhna played an important role in the early developments which led to the eventual emergence of a centralized Jewish communal organization in Poland.

Among Rabbi Shakhna's greatest accomplishments was the yeshivah which he founded at Lublin about 1520. The school attracted students from all parts of the country, and from abroad. The scholarly fame of the rosh yeshivah was, of course, an important factor. Additional factors were the large city of Lublin, located in the very center of the country, and the wealth of Rabbi Shakhna's family which enabled him to support needy students generously. Most important, however, was the fact that Shakhna, the greatest among Jacob Pollack's disciples, had the best command of his method of study, the Pilpul.

To be sure, some historians believe that Rabbi Shakhna was committed to the method of Pilpul to a lesser degree than his teacher. They point out that in the yeshivah of Lublin, Talmud, where the Pilpul mainly finds its application, was not the only subject of study. Much time and attention were devoted to the study of the codes of law, which lend themselves much less to "pilpulizing." Rabbi Shakhna thus led his school in the middle of the road, between the purely theoretical Pilpul and the practical Halakhah.

Rabbi Shakhna trained his pupils in the practice of working out opinions in concrete legal cases. He manifested a clear tendency to leave the final decision to the individual rabbi before whom a problem was actually brought, since he alone could be totally familiar with all the facts. Shakhna himself courageously issued legal opinions which won the approval of only a handful of the contemporary rabbis. His pupils were so impressed with his alacrity in applying the theoretical Halakhah to concrete cases that they implored him to write a systematic code of the laws of what is forbidden and what is permissible (*isur weheter*).

It is equally true, however, that Shakhna's method of arriving at a legal opinion was the Pilpul. In one of his opinions, printed during his lifetime (1540), the title page bears the remark that its validity was proved by the author "through a great pilpul." The greatest of Shakhna's pupils, his son-in-law Moses Isserles, relates that Rabbi Shakhna once issued a legal opinion which was severely criticized by almost the entire rabbinate. The opponents charged that he plunged so deeply into a pilpul, that it was impossible to follow him. We thus see that Rabbi Shakhna was fully committed to the Pilpul method and gave it a dominant position in his school. The fact that the publisher of the above-mentioned legal opinion saw fit to indicate on the title page that it is based on a "great pilpul" testifies to the popularity of the new method.

The practical need to study the codes of law and the desire

to arrive at a deeper understanding of Talmudic texts were responsible for the use of three great works as textbooks in the yeshivah of Lublin: The *Mordecai,* the *Commentary on the Talmud by* Asher ben Jehiel, and the *Arbaah Turim (The Four Rows).* The *Mordecai* is a broadly conceived halakhic work authored by Rabbi Mordecai ben Hillel Hacohen, a great scholar who perished in Nuremberg together with his wife and five children during the Rindfleish riots in the year 1298. In his work he generally presents the Franco-German Talmudic scholars' opinions on the religious law. It seems that when he was martyred the author had not yet decided upon a name for his work. Posterity simply named the book after its author. The fact that Rabbi Mordecai always carefully identified his sources made his work an ideal anthology for use in yeshivahs. The regard which Polish Jewry had for the Franco-German Talmudic scholars, who were its religio-cultural "ancestors," made the *Mordecai* doubly popular in Poland's Rabbinic colleges.

The other two works were written by Rabbi Asher and his son Jacob, respectively, both among medieval Germany's foremost Jewish scholars. Contemporaries of Rabbi Mordecai, they escaped to Spain in time to avoid the latter's fate. In 1305 Rabbi Asher was appointed chief rabbi of the city of Toledo. He held this post until his death in 1328. His son Jacob also lived in Toledo. Jacob devoted most of his time to research. The writings of both father and son are among the most important Talmudic works produced in the Middle Ages. The son's *Arbaah Turim* is a systematically arranged and complete code of the Jewish law, which became the foundation for the compilation of the definitive code of Jewish law, the *Shulhan Arukh (The Prepared Table),* more than two hundred years later. Though Asher and Jacob spent a considerable part of their life among the Jews of Spain, their works, nevertheless, basically represent the Franco-German tradition of Jewish scholarship.

Still another textbook, *Shaare Dura (The Gates of Dueren)* won an important place in the yeshivah of Lublin. This volume, written by Isaac of Dueren, is mostly concerned with describing the dietary laws. It was intended as a textbook for the author's pupils. Published at Cracow in 1534, it is perhaps the first Hebrew book ever printed in Poland. Rabbi Shakhna either exploited the fact that the book was published and the students could acquire it easily and cheaply, or perhaps the book was printed because the demand for it among the students of the yeshivahs was great.

The number of students in Shakhna's school was considerable. Many of them were sons of aristocratic families. Outstanding among them was Moses Isserles, a son of one of the wealthiest Jews in Cracow. Shakhna offered his daughter Golda, named after his mother, to Moses in marriage. Another of Shakhna's pupils was Hayim ben Bezalel, a native of Posen and a brother of Prague's most famous rabbi, Judah Loew. Hayim relates that he was trained in several yeshivahs in Poland, but acquired most of his knowledge at the school of "the wondrous gaon Rabbi Shakhna, of blessed memory." Moses Isserles recalled that all the leading scholars of Poland were Shakhna's pupils. Curiously, some of Shakhna's pupils often criticized his legal opinions. Nevertheless, admiration for their teacher knew no limits. Shakhna's forceful personality no doubt made an indelible impression upon his students.

Of major significance was the emphasis Rabbi Shakhna put in his legal opinions on the new religious usage (*minhag*) as it began to unfold in Poland's rising Jewish community. He even considered it more valid than the opinions of the revered Franco-German scholars. The Jews of Poland accepted Shakhna's opinions even though they were controversial. Several decades after his death, the Jewish community of Cracow introduced certain regulations in Jewish marriage law in accordance with opinions issued by him.

During the times of Rabbi Shakhna the study of Torah was stimulated by the establishment of Hebrew printing presses in Poland. Until 1530 not a single Hebrew book was published there. Books were imported from Italy, the cradle of the printed Hebrew book, and from Prague. In the early thirties

of the sixteenth century the three Helitz brothers began to print
Hebrew books in Cracow. Their name suggests their origin was
Halicz in Southeastern Poland. The type they used in their
press indicates that they probably learned their art in Prague.
The first book they published was the already mentioned
Shaare Dura. This work, as we have seen, is a reference book
designed for the use of yeshivah students. A year or two later
they published *Mirkebeth Hamishne (The Second Chariot)*, also
known under the name *Sepher shel Rabbi Anshel (Anshel's Book)*,
which was of great importance to the general public. This book,
about whose author little is known, is a Hebrew-Yiddish dictionary
which enables the average person to study the Bible independently.

At first the new publishing house gave promise of becoming
a great cultural factor in Poland's Jewish community. However,
in 1537 the Helitz brothers converted to Christianity. We do
not know what prompted the Cracow printers to abandon their
ancestral faith. But it is obvious that the Jews no longer had
use for Jewish religious books published by the renegades. The
printers, however, did not give in. Knowing that the Jews were
their only prospective customers, they persuaded the king to
force Jews to buy their books. In order to be sure that the Jews
would comply with his order, the king also granted the converts an exclusive monopoly over the importation of Hebrew
books from abroad. Nevertheless, the stranglehold on the
Jewish book market granted to the converts was unsuccessful.
The Jews boycotted the book business of the Helitz brothers
and probably satisfied their need for Hebrew books by im-
porting them clandestinely. Finally, the king forced the three
leading communities of Cracow, Posen, and Lemberg to buy
from the converts all the books they had in stock. The Jews,
of course, were forced to comply. The extreme rarity of the
books published by the Helitz brothers today suggests that
the communities destroyed the acquired stock. The converts
finally surrendered and stopped printing Hebrew books. Some
time later one of them went to Constantinople, returned to
Judaism, and as a repentant again began to publish Rabbinic
books.

About a score of years passed before the printing of Hebrew books in Poland was resumed. The new press was established in Lublin shortly before Rabbi Shakhna's death. And here, at the new printing press, a very ambitious project was begun: the publication of the first Polish edition of the Talmud. There were, it seems, some doubts whether Polish Jewry, not yet very large in number, would be in a position to finance a project of this magnitude. Help came from the rabbis and from the heads of yeshivahs in the three main provinces of the Commonwealth: Poland, the Ukraine, and Lithuania. They issued a recommendation that all the yeshivahs should offer courses in the same tractate of the Talmud each semester and that this tractate should then be published by the Lublin printers. In the following semester another tractate should be selected as a universally studied subject and be published. In this manner the rabbis hoped to secure the publication of the complete Talmud. The decision of the rabbis, originally motivated by financial reasons, had a much greater effect on the scholarly world than could have been foreseen. The result was not only a means of facilitating the publication of the Talmud, but also the first common action of the entire Jewish community in the field of the study of Torah. A few decades later, when the Council of the Four Lands was instituted, regulation on a national basis of matters pertaining to Jewish education and scholarship achieved the status of a generally recognized practice. The newly established custom also made it easy for wandering scholars to transfer from one yeshivah to another without interrupting their studies. In addition, it stimulated discussions among rabbinic writers by constantly focusing their interest on similar themes.

The first tractate to be published in Lublin was *Shevuoth* (Oaths). It came off the press late in 1558, the year of Shakhna's death. It is possible that when the book was published he was no longer alive. It is certain, however, that he participated in the preparations for the publication of the Talmud. Several tractates of this edition were printed, according to their title page, from a text he edited.

Rabbi Shakhna's literary heritage is negligible. The only works that he left are a few legal opinions, mainly in the field of marriage law. It is not improbable that some unnoticed old manuscripts kept in the libraries contain additional writings by Rabbi Shakhna. But it is certain that he never wrote comprehensive works. The most illustrious of his students, Moses Isserles, remarked that Shakhna wrote his opinions in a concise style and presented his arguments in accordance with the Pilpul method. Shakhna's son says that he and other scholars urged Shakhna to write a code of laws. His answer, prompted by his great piety and humility, for he was the most modest of men, was: "I know that the rabbis would henceforth render decisions only in accordance with what I have written, since the law always follows the latter decisions, and I have no desire that all should rely on me." The memory of the son retained, of course, mainly the fact that his father was a pious and humble man. But other sources relate that Rabbi Shakhna was far from being humble when he had to make a decision. He had the courage to interpret certain passages in the Talmud in a fashion conflicting with the commentary of Rashi, the universally accepted authority. In fact, most of the time his interpretations and opinions evoked the opposition of his contemporaries and his own disciples.

Jacob Pollack's and Shakhna's failure to give their teachings a literary form possibly resulted from the fact that they lived during the formative period of Torah learning in Poland. This was an epoch when public opinion in the field of Torah learning was just beginning to emerge in the country. There was not yet the proper literary atmosphere to stimulate scholars to become authors. Both Jacob Pollack and Shalom Shakhna realized the great potentialities for training a generation of native scholars. They devoted all their skill and all their energy to this task. Another reason why they did not produce literary works lies in the character of the Pilpul. Pilpul is basically an oral discipline, in which the lively discussion heats the fantasy and stimulates the participants. However, once one begins to impose a literary form upon it, much of its original brilliance and excitement is lost. Its two great protagonists, therefore, left only the memory of their keen thought in Jewish jurisprudence as their heritage. Later, in times quite close to our own generation, some of the most illustrious Talmudic sages refrained from writing down their teachings, choosing to leave to posterity only a great legend.

In November, 1558, Rabbi Shakhna died in Lublin. On his grave a tombstone was placed with a long inscription telling of his greatness. Several decades ago the tombstone, corroded by time, was replaced by a new one. Pious Jews observed a custom of frequently visiting his grave.

CHAPTER FOUR

THE AGE OF THE RAMA AND THE MAHARSHAL

I.

After Rabbi Shakhna's death, Cracow was restored as the main center of Torah learning. This seat of learning developed around the great personality of Rabbi Moses Isserles, known as the Rama. Isserles, Shakhna's son-in-law, was also one of his most brilliant pupils.

It was a favorable time for Torah study to flourish. Polish Jewry then enjoyed economic prosperity and had the means to support new intellectual aspirations. Also the general climate in Poland at large was favorable to spiritual development. It was a time when the Protestant movement and the culture of the Renaissance became widespread, mainly amongst the Polish aristocracy. A spirit of cultural freedom, characteristic of the new movement, was also strongly represented in Jewish society. The last Yagellonian, Sigismund August (1548–1572), warmly supported the humanist movement. He collected a large valuable library. In his time Polish literature began to blossom. This was also a time when literature began to flourish among the Commonwealth's Jews.

Relations between the Jews of Poland and their co-religionists in Italy, the center of the culture of the Renaissance, were quite close. These years may be characterized as a time when the Polish intellectual world liberated itself from centuries-old German influences and began to relate more to Italy. Aristocratic young men studied at Italian universities. The taste of the Italian Renaissance pervaded Polish literature and architecture during the second part of the century. A similar interest in Italy was discernible among Polish Jews. Many immigrants from Germany had relatives among the German Jews in Northern Italy. The relations between the rabbis of the two countries were also very close. The Italian influence upon Polish Jewry was, therefore, quite intense. Many positive as well as negative characteristics of Italian Renaissance Jewry appeared in Poland and served as a background for the Polish Jewish culture of that era. Thus Poland's fledgling Hebrew literature often employed the sharp polemical style used by "Men of the Renaissance" to subdue and ridicule their opponents. Even a scholar of the calibre of Rabbi Solomon Luria attacked his opponents in a remarkably caustic manner. His struggles often remind us of the heated clashes among Italian Jewish humanists. But the anonymous humanist, who, in 1559, wrote a pamphlet against the rabbi of Posen, surpassed his most hotheaded Italian colleagues by far in his use of his vast erudition in Jewish literature and his mastery of the Hebrew language in abusing his opponent with a remarkable selection of insults.

A great desire developed among contemporary Jews in Poland to obtain rabbinic ordination, *semikhah*, quite in the fashion of the Italian Jews. When the famous Spanish-Jewish statesman and thinker Don Isaac Abravanel arrived in Italy some fifty years earlier, he became aware of the universal craving for the *semikhah*. It appears, Abravanel complained, as if the Jews are copying the Gentiles' eagerness to get the title "doctor." Solomon Luria similarly complained, with the exaggeration of a bitter man, that since in Poland everybody wanted the title of a rabbi, the ordained are many but the learned are few.

The noble qualities of the Jews of the Renaissance also penetrated Poland. A genuine intellectual interest emerged among the Jewish aristocracy. Rabbi Shakhna was the son of a magnate, as were also Rabbi Moses Isserles and his brother-in-law Rabbi Joseph Katz, a rosh yeshivah in Cracow. They all spent a considerable share of their wealth in maintaining their schools and students. The always bitter Solomon Luria accused the rich yeshivah heads of using their money to attract students. He failed to perceive the important role of these yeshivah maecenases in promoting Torah learning in Poland. That Torah learning was dear to the entire Jewish aristocracy is illustrated by the activities of Isaac May of Lublin, a popular physician, and a great benefactor of Lublin's Jewish community. He once acquired a piece of land from a Gentile which he then offered to the community as a site for a yeshivah, a synagogue, and a hospital. The communal yeshivah was built on this land. Its head was to be, according to a royal decree, of higher rank than the other rabbis and heads of the other yeshivahs. (See below.)

Under Italian impact the printing of Hebrew books further expanded. In 1568 a certain Isaac of Prostitz, an Italian arrival, was granted a permit by King Sigismund August to open a Hebrew printing press in Cracow. During the last three decades of the century, with only a short interruption caused by intrigues of the Catholic clergy, he published many important Hebrew works. The Lublin printers, too, employed typesetters from Italy. The books printed in Cracow by the Helitz brothers in the thirties vividly resemble in their appearance the contemporary products of the German printing presses. The Cracow and Lublin publications of the sixties and seventies clearly reveal the impact of Renaissance Italy in their type and title pages.

The hunger for Hebrew books in Poland now became so intense that, simultaneously with the increased production of the local printing presses, large numbers of books had to be imported from Italy. The imports reached such dimensions, however, that they became a menace to the local book industry. Consequently, the Jewish communal authorities had to intervene both to secure a proper supply of books and at the same time to protect the interests of Cracow's and Lublin's publishing houses.

II.

A scrutiny of the rabbinic profession in Poland at the mid-century reveals that the number of immigrant rabbis was still considerable. Posen, for example, still largely depended upon such immigrant rabbis. We also find immigrants among the yeshivah heads. The number of native scholars, however, was increasing to such a degree, that some of the learned immigrants from Germany were unable to obtain positions and had to return to their former home.

An impressive interest in learning also appeared among people who did not belong to the professional intelligentsia. Moses Isserles relates that it was customary to discuss learned subjects during festive meals. A scholar who immigrated to Italy at the end of the century recalled that in Cracow even the butchers were learned men. The increased interest in learning manifested by laymen created a need for a digest literature that would be in keeping with the limited time available to them for study. Moses Isserles tells us that the law book *Shaare-Dura*, by Isaac of Dueren, so popular in Rabbi Shakhna's yeshivah, was also now in great demand because of its conciseness. In general, Isserles asserted, his generation preferred to study from abridged texts. Actually, already earlier in the century such tendencies prompted Rabbi Shakhna's students to plead with him to write a code of laws. In the field of Jewish jurisprudence a systematic code of laws always constituted a means for abridged study. The following episode will illustrate how boundless the demand for abridged law books was. Rabbi Hayim ben Bezalel, a fine scholar and brilliant writer, prepared a manuscript containing an abridged catalogue of the Jewish religious laws for his own reference. When his students learned of it, they secretly removed the manuscript and copied it for themselves. When Rabbi Hayim became aware of what had happened, he ordered them to return his book together with its copies. He was of the opinion that yeshivah students should not study from such abridged textbooks.

In the yeshivahs Jewish law was taught in a thorough manner despite the predilection for abridgements. More and more young men entered the yeshivahs. Economic prosperity and the increased intellectual interest did their share in drawing many

young men to the schools of higher learning. The popularity
of the schools further increased because of the broad, judicial
autonomy enjoyed by the Jews. The need for people trained in
Jewish civil law was great, and this subject became a major
field of study in the schools. The number of yeshivahs increased. Each of the big cities, such as Cracow, Lublin, Posen,
and Lemberg, had a yeshivah, sometimes several. We are told
that once, in Cracow, when the students of a certain yeshivah
were dissatisfied with its head, they left the school and established a new one in the same neighborhood.

In the sixties attempts were made to establish yeshivahs of
a very high status, akin to universities. This, it seems, could be
achieved by obtaining a special royal patent that would expli-
cate the status of the institution and of its head. Such a royal
patent was granted in 1571 to one of the rabbis of Lemberg.
He was given the right to open yeshivahs in all of the cities of
the kingdom. In addition, he was given complete jurisdiction
over the student body, which he was to exert in accordance
with Jewish law. The highest rank was granted by King Sigismund August in 1567 to the new communal school built in
Lublin on land acquired for this purpose by Dr. Isaac May.
The royal document permitted the head of the yeshivah to be
invested with the proud title of "rector," commonly used by
heads of the universities. Like them he was freed from paying
taxes and in addition was exempted from the authority of the
rabbi, who at that time was Israel, Shakhna's son. The school
was established with communal funds. Much care was given
to make the building as comfortable for the students as possible.
There was free tuition. The head of the school was to be elected
from among and by all of the rabbis and scholars of the city.
This, of course, resembles the fashion by which a rector is
elected by all faculties of the university.

This was a time when many young Christian men left the
little towns to study at the Jagiellonian University in Cracow.
Similarly, young Jews from small towns and villages were
going in large numbers to yeshivahs in the large cities. Among
the Jews, however, the proportion of students surpassed by far

that of Christians who studied at the universities. Often small towns sent the young men to the yeshivahs in groups, supervised by specially hired adults.

The academic year in the yeshivahs commenced in the fall, about the beginning of the month of Heshwan. The main subject studied in the yeshivahs was, of course, the Talmud. We shall see further that the major part of Hebrew books written at the time in Poland was in the field of Talmudic studies. We are told that the chief rabbi of Posen recommended, in a sermon in 1559, that everybody should study only the Talmud, even if it caused the neglect of the Bible. When one observes all that was happening in the intellectual life of Polish Jewry at that time, one is easily persuaded that the demand of the rabbi of Posen expressed the feelings of the great majority.

In line with the interest in study, an urge for literary creativity emerged. It is impossible to explain why Poland's Jewish community, which could look back on a history of several centuries, did not produce a single literary work until the sixteenth century. It will be recalled that during the second part of the fifteenth century, Moses the "Exile," a prolific writer, lived in Kiev. Still, no scholar in the not-too distant Lemberg and Lublin was inspired to literary activity by him. It is also difficult to understand why the immigrant rabbinic authors from Germany did not manifest any literary interest once they came to Poland. Jacob Pollack and Shalom Shakhna wrote a negligible number of rabbinic responsa. Obviously, no "literary atmosphere" existed among Poland's Jews. By the middle of the century, however, a decisive change occurred. It was as if a long dormant literary force suddenly broke loose. It became so fashionable to write books that even several ritual slaughterers took to the pen and wrote handbooks describing the laws and rules of their profession. Some of these, incidentally, became the standard works in their field. The contemporary sources list an impressive catalogue of rabbinic authors who wrote works in various fields of Jewish learning. The true character of this literary epoch, however, is manifested in the works of the rabbi and rosh yeshivah of Cracow, Moses Isserles, known as Rama, and his somewhat older contemporary and friend, Solomon Luria, the Maharshal.

III.

Rabbi Moses Isserles was a scion of one of Cracow's wealthiest families. A family of recent immigrants from Germany, it came to occupy an influential position in the community in a comparatively short time. Moses' father, Israel Isserl, was a learned man and a widely known financier. His business transactions reached the royal court. Isserl evinced a deep interest in public life and was, it seems, one of the leaders of the community.

The exact date of Moses' birth is unknown. It will be correct to assume that he was born about 1520. As a young lad he went to Lublin to study under Rabbi Shakhna and quickly won the fame as brilliant scholar. Equally phenomenal were his diligence and perseverance. In the many works that Isserles wrote later in his life he shows the superb erudition in the vast sea of Jewish literature that can be acquired only by an assiduous student. Young Moses returned to Cracow not later than 1547 and was appointed to the post of the rabbi. His appointment was confirmed by a royal patent. The range of his authority, however, was not as wide as that of Rabbi Jacob Pollack and Rabbi Shalom Shakhna. At that time, or perhaps earlier in Lublin, Moses married Rabbi Shakhna's daughter Golda.

A short time after his return to Cracow, Rabbi Moses Isserles founded a yeshivah. The school gained fame quite rapidly and attracted many students. It seems that some even came from as far as West Germany. We do not know what had happened to the yeshivah opened earlier in Cracow by Jacob Pollack after its founder left the city. We may assume it was either closed or it lost its significance. Nor could the yeshivah established in Cracow about 1540 and headed by Rabbi Joseph Katz, compete in importance with the yeshivah of Lublin. With the opening of Moses Isserles' new school, Cracow again became a great center of Torah learning.

The appointment of Moses Isserles at a very young age as rabbi and rosh yeshivah in a major community such as Cracow put him in a somewhat embarrassing position. Some of the older, recognized scholars revealed a certain degree of impatience in their learned correspondence with him. German Jewish scholars, especially, viewed with envy the young man, who in no time managed to create a new, prominent Ashkenazic center of learning. To be sure, Moses Isserles himself felt that the crown was put on his head too early: "I was still very young," he writes, "I have not kept my own vineyard yet, and already I have been appointed to show the way to others. . . ." It did not take long, however, and people began to forget that the rabbi of Cracow was a young man. Moses' fame as a rosh yeshivah, a jurist, and a thinker spread so widely that he was considered one of the greatest men of his generation.

Moses Isserles held his positions of rabbi and rosh-yeshivah for a full quarter of a century. He was very much influenced by the culture of the Renaissance. But he was not the quarrelsome man of the type of Jacob Pollack and Rabbi Shakhna, his teacher and father-in-law. He led a quiet, peaceful life, devoted to his students and to the composition of his great works. Suddenly, in the years 1551 and 1552 disaster struck. In a short time his wife Golda at age twenty, his mother, and also his grandmother all succumbed to an epidemic. In 1556 a new epidemic drove him out of his home and he spent the usually joyous holiday of Purim in loneliness, far from his family. Apparently there were no more crises in his later years. He later married a sister of the above-mentioned Rabbi Joseph Katz. The father, Isserl, had continued success in his business activities, and the wealth of the family permitted Moses to properly care for the needs of his students. At that time the Jews of Cracow were in great need of a new synagogue, but no permit for its erection could be obtained due to the opposition of the Catholic clergy. Isserl, however, succeeded in removing all obstacles and built a synagogue which he dedicated

to the memory of his wife. This house of worship, known as
the Rama Shul, although small, is great in historic significance.
It survived the destruction of Cracow's Jewish community during the Nazi holocaust.

Rabbi Moses Isserles died on *Lag Baomer* 1572. He was
buried in Cracow's old Jewish cemetery, a short distance from
the synagogue bearing his name. Later generations wove many
legends around the personality of the beloved and revered master. One legend has it that the great rabbi, who died on the
thirty-third day of counting the *omer,* lived only thirty-three
years, authored thirty-three works, and was eulogized at his
funeral for his thirty-three virtues. According to other legends
he was even a miracle worker. Masses of Jews used to visit
his grave every *Lag Baomer* down to our own times.

IV.

Rabbi Moses' extraordinary popularity with his contemporaries was due to his fame as a great scholar and saintly man.
The old minute book of the Jewish burial society of Cracow
relates that he was very lavish in giving charity. He was especially generous in his support of orphans and widows.
Through him the custom of contributing to the poor for mat-
zoth for Passover (*Maoth hittim,* wheat money), began to be
universally practiced and attained the status of an important
law. His compassion and courage manifested themselves on a
certain Friday when an orphaned girl was to be married and a
conflict about the dowry threatened to postpone the wedding.
He feared that if the ceremony were postponed, the wedding
would be cancelled. He, therefore, ordered that the Friday
night service be delayed for an hour and a half until the differences were settled and the orphan was married. To be sure,
his action drew sharp criticism from many of his contemporaries. But Rabbi Moses remained convinced that under no
circumstances should the happiness of a poor orphan be jeop-
ardized.

When Rabbi Moses Isserles' contemporaries considered his personality and read his books, they discovered a great resemblance between him and Moses Maimonides. This comparison was perpetuated in an engraving on his tombstone: *Mimosheh wead Mosheh lo kam Beyisrael Kemosheh,* From Moses (Maimonides) to Moses (Isserles) there was no greater man in Israel than Moses (Isserles). Indeed, it was obvious to everybody that Isserles admired the "Great Eagle" and endeavored to walk in his ways. Like Maimonides, Isserles too wrote halakhic and philosophical works. He was well versed in the Jewish philosophical literature of the Middle Ages, and his interest in the sciences greatly surpassed that of his colleagues in the Polish rabbinate. He justified his plan to compose an allegorical commentary to the laws on the sacrifices by the argument that Maimonides did the same. It is quite likely that when Isserles divided his main philosophical work, *Torath Haolah (The Law of the Burnt Offering),* into three parts, he endeavored to structure it after Maimonides' *Guide of the Perplexed.*

As an adherent of Maimonidean teachings, Rabbi Moses Isserles used his impressive erudition in the sciences in discussing problems of the *halakhah.* He also declared it permissible to study the sciences at times that are not usually devoted to the study of Torah. At the same time he was strongly attracted to the teachings of Jewish mysticism and wrote a commentary on the *Zohar, The Book of Splendor,* often called the Bible of the kabalists. When he studied the Scriptures he looked for the deeper ideas that are hidden, as he believed, under the surface of the text. He tried to fuse all these sometimes conflicting tendencies into a harmonious system. True, he challenged the opinions of the rabbis with arguments borrowed from the sciences; but he always found a way to reconcile them ultimately. He also drew upon the aggadic elements in the Talmud for ideas about Man and the Universe.

Rabbi Moses Isserles presented his views on God, the Universe, and Man, and on the relationship between man's free thought and his duty to believe, in two works: *Mehir Yayin, Substitution for Wine,* an allegoric commentary on the Book of

Esther, and the above-mentioned *Torath Haolah,* a similar commentary on the sacrifices. *Mehir Yayin* is a small treatise that Isserles wrote on a certain Purim day when an epidemic drove him out of Cracow. Unable to celebrate the customary joyful Purim feast, he wrote the little book in a few short hours, as a "substitution" for the banquet. On *Torath Haolah,* however, he worked many years as is fitting for a comprehensive work in theology and philosophy. Both works are nevertheless closely related and are designed to make known his basic philosophical views.

Isserles' views on the foundations of Judaism and on the purpose of man's life seem to lack originality. He rarely introduced new thoughts that great thinkers had not presented before. He believed that the purpose of man in this world is to endeavor to understand all that surrounds him. It is man's duty to believe fully in *creatio ex nihilo,* in the unity of God, in the divine origin of the Torah, and in reward and punishment. Besides this, however, it is also his duty to attempt to grasp the meaning of these concepts, by way of meditation. When man arrives at a profound understanding of the Torah and of all its hidden secrets, he will attain Divine inspiration, the greatest gift that can be granted to him in this world. Isserles arrived at these opinions not by simply borrowing them from the medieval Jewish philosophers. He rather worked his way up to them by his own effort. Isserles' philosophical writings lack the logic and clarity of formulation that we find in the works of the Spanish-Jewish philosophers. His works do not reveal the clear structure that results from a logical presentation of a system of thoughts. Isserles lived in a country devoid of an atmosphere of philosophical thinking, unlike the situation that existed in the Mediterranean Jewish communities during the epoch of Judeo-Arabic symbiosis. Not having the proper philosophical schooling, he created for himself the means, involved as they may have been, to find his way to his Weltanshauung. The main fault with his philosophical writings lies in his effort to squeeze them into an artificial framework of allegorical interpretations. He preferred to employ this method because he was anxious to make sure not only that his ideas did not contradict the Bible and the opinions of the sages of the Talmud, but that they also could be directly validated from these sources. Consequently, he often permitted himself, in fact too often, to be dragged into the fantastic, boundless world of the allegory. In the treatise *Mehir Yayin* the phrase "From India even unto Ethiopia" (Esther I) "India" represents man's birth and "Ethiopia" the day of his death. In *Torath Haolah*, lengthy discourses describe how the Temple in Jerusalem and the holy vessels symbolize the Torah and all the worlds. Many stories of the Torah and many of the precepts, including the Sabbath, are meant to prove one single concept—namely, that God created the world out of nothing.

Though the allegorical method led Isserles again and again into charmed and fantastic labyrinths, *Torath Haolah* remains basically a philosophical work, in which its author made a heroic effort to systematically clarify, in his own way, the main problems that are of concern to the thinking and believing man. The book is filled with ideas borrowed from Maimonides. There is hardly a page on which the *Guide of the Perplexed* is not quoted. Isserles knew and quoted many other medieval Jewish philosophers as well. To be sure, his exclusive sources were the writings of the *Jewish* philosophers. To study what non-Jewish thinkers had to say about God and the Universe, was beyond the boundaries he permitted himself. He believed that only leisure time could be devoted even to the study of the Jewish philosophers and scientists. His ultimate conviction was that only in the Torah could absolute truth be found, and that only in the Scriptures could man find an answer to all his questions.

Despite the importance Moses Isserles ascribed to his philosophical studies, he was basically and foremost a *lamdan,* that is, a rabbi who devoted his talent, time, and enthusiasm to the study of the Talmud and the Halakhah in their practical application to the needs of the Jewish community. It should be assumed that his preoccupation with philosophical studies added splendor to his stature. Still the greatest tribute was given to him as a jurist, and as a jurist, not as a philosopher, he won for himself an important place in the history of the Jewish people.

A review of the halakhic writings of Rabbi Moses Isserles reveals that they all center around the two textbooks popular in the yeshivahs: *Shaare Dura* and *Arbaa Turim*. Obviously, Isserles' literary work was closely tied to his activities as rosh yeshivah. Isserles was aware of the great popularity of *Shaare Dura* among the academic youth and lay intelligentsia. But he was not fully satisfied with this frequently reprinted textbook. He thought that the conciseness of its style, so attractive to the students, limited its usefulness. In addition, he was convinced that the book had become somewhat antiquated during the one hundred and fifty years following its composition. All that time Jewish jurisprudence had discussed the dietary laws, the main subject of *Shaare Dura,* in manifold ways. Isserles therefore wrote his *Torath Hatath, The Law of the Sin Offering,* in which he rearranged the material of *Shaare Dura* in a more popular vein and brought it up to date. Here and there he wrote additions to the original text to make it more explicit. He also offered a "final conclusion" to each particular law, based on later research.

Of major importance is the work Rabbi Moses Isserles did on the *Arbaa Turim*. He tells us that he long planned to select one of the important older codes of Jewish law and supplement it with the opinions of the later scholars on the various laws. In other words, he planned to author an halakhic encyclopedia that could be easily used as a reference book by every rabbi confronted with the need of rendering a decision. After much consideration he decided to use as a basis for his work the code *Arbaa Turim* which practically every rabbi studied during his years of training. In the 1550's, when Isserles had completed part of the work, Rabbi Joseph Karo, a great scholar in the Holy Land, published his book under the name *Beth Yoseph,* which was an encyclopedia of the type planned by Isserles. This work, too, was arranged around the code *Arbaa Turim*. Isserles was disappointed. He believed that it was the will of Heaven that Karo, not himself, compose the definitive halakhic code. Curiously, the folk-legend took cognizance of the "race" between the greatest jurist among Near-Eastern Jewry and the greatest jurist among the Ashkenazim. It tells that Rabbi Joseph Karo's *maggid*, "Preacher" (an invisible messenger from Heaven that often visited him, as he believed), revealed to him secretly that a work similar to his *Beth Yoseph* was being written in Cracow, and that he should therefore hasten the publication of his book. Joseph Karo heeded the advice of his "familiar spirit" and won the race with Moses Isserles.

The initial disappointment of Rabbi Moses Isserles was overwhelming. But when he put the *Beth Yoseph* to a closer analysis, he discovered that there still remained much for him to do. He realized that Rabbi Joseph Karo was generally guided exclusively by the opinions of the Sephardic scholars, but passed over in silence the teachings of the Ashkenazic rabbis. Consequently, Rabbi Moses resumed his research and completed the work which he named *Darkhe Mosheh, The Ways of Moses*. However, he was forced to give the book a different structure from that originally planned. Instead of adding a broad, comprehensive commentary to *Arbaa Turim*, *Darkhe Mosheh* became a critique and a supplement to *Beth Yoseph*. No doubt, in its new form Isserles' work lost very much from a literary point of view. But it later became the starting point for another great work of Moses Isserles, in connection with which destiny again entangled him with the work of Joseph Karo.

Several years after the publication of *Beth Yoseph*, Rabbi Joseph Karo completed and published his famous, and to this day universally accepted, Jewish code of laws, *Shulhan Arukh*. In this work Joseph Karo presented a systematic arrangement of all Jewish laws, derived from the material available in *Arbaa Turim* and his own lengthy commentary *Beth Yoseph*. A comparison of the *Shulhan Arukh* and *Arbaa Turim* shows how step by step the definite Jewish code of laws came into being. Rabbi Jacob ben Asher drew from the vast sea of the Talmud the legal material that he found in it and arranged it according to its subject-matter. But *Arbaa Turim*, the result of his work, cannot be termed a regular code of laws. Jacob ben Asher interspersed only too often the formulations of the various laws with statements of the Tannaim and Amoraim. In the *Shulhan Arukh* Rabbi Joseph Karo eliminated all these statements and, instead, presented the laws in short, clearly formulated paragraphs, appropriate to a code of laws. In addition, as we have seen, he utilized the opinions of later scholars of the Sephardic world, mostly those of Maimonides.

As soon as the *Shulhan Arukh* came off the press, it started a veritably triumphant march through the Jewish world. Everybody realized that finally a code of laws in the true sense of the word was now available as a guide for the Jews' daily life. To be sure, some of the leading scholars looked askance at the new work. They feared that a "petrification" of the Halakhah and a diminution of the study of the Talmud would result. It was basically the same fear that raised its head four centuries earlier when Maimonides composed his *Mishneh Torah,* also a code of laws. In later chapters it will be seen how at the turn of the century, especially in Poland, the struggle provoked by the *Shulhan Arukh* gained momentum. But the advantages of the code were so obvious that the Jewish people accepted it enthusiastically despite the objections of scholarly and saintly men.

At the time of the publication of the *Shulhan Arukh,* Jewish jurisprudence in Poland was dominated by Rabbi Solomon Luria and Rabbi Moses Isserles. We shall see later that Solomon Luria was the type of scholar for whom a deep and thorough analysis of concepts was the most important task of research. He, naturally, considered a book such as the *Shulhan Arukh* superfluous and even damaging. He therefore led a sharp attack against the new code of laws. Moses Isserles, however, was by nature very much interested in such a work. He was clearly impressed by the predilection of both the academic youth and the lay intelligentsia for digest literature. Had not Joseph Karo won the literary "race" with him, Isserles himself would have inevitably arrived at the composition of a code of laws. Thus in the manner in which he earlier added his corrections to the *Beth Yosef*, he now proceeded to supplement the *Shulhan Arukh*.

The supplement which Rabbi Moses Isserles wrote to the *Shulhan Arukh* he named *Mappah, The Table Cloth*. By naming his work in this way, he wanted to say that according to him Joseph Karo's "Prepared Table" still lacked a "Table Cloth," and that only after his "Cloth" was spread over the "Table" would the benefit derived from it be complete. Originally Isserles probably planned to publish his *Mappah* either as a separate book or in the editions of the *Shulhan Arukh*, at its side, in the manner in which Karo's *Beth Yoseph* was printed in the standard editions of *Arbaa Turim*. The *Mappah*, however, turned out to be so organically intertwined with the *Shulhan Arukh* that it began to be printed within the text of the latter. The use of two types of print is the means by which the texts of the two books are distinguishable. The notes of Moses Isserles sometimes have for their purpose the clarification of Joseph Karo's formulations. This, however, is not their avowed task. The main task is to correct the *Shulhan Arukh* in order to bring it in line with the usage of Ashkenazic Jewry. The title page of the first edition states clearly that the notes contained in the *Mappah* offer laws and customs "from all areas of Ashkenaz." Generally, Isserles introduced in his critical notes three innovations: he superimposed *the minhag Ashkenaz*, the Ashkenazic custom on the Sephardic *Shulhan Arukh;* he stressed the opinions of the scholars of the immediately preceding generations (*aharonim*); and among the scholars of former generations he gave precedence to the opinions of the Tosaphists. Isserles' main achievement in the *Mappah* lies in the fact that even average scholars who were not familiar with the different halakhic trends of the various parts of the Jewish people were now in a position to use the *Shulhan Arukh* independently as a guide for their everyday life. The *Shulhan Arukh* became a true folk book for both major parts of the Jewish people. We will see later how this code of laws was under fire for a long time. But all the attacks could not shatter the solid base that Moses Isserles built for it within Ashkenazic Jewry. When, several decades after Isserles' death, everybody recognized this fact, a number of great scholars in Poland "surrounded" the *Shulhan Arukh* with a wreath of basic commentaries, and in this form it was accepted with finality by Eastern European Jewry. The story of the dramatic struggle around the position of the *Shulhan Arukh* will occupy us in some of the later chapters.

V.

The character and contents of Moses Isserles' works provide a fairly clear picture of his position and attitudes as a *possek,* a codifier of the Jewish law. His teaching and literary work were dedicated to the ideal of helping the individual Jew and the Jewish community to conduct their Jewish life in accordance with the Halakhah. In his school Isserles trained rabbis for the communities, and his works served as reference books for the use of the rabbis and learned laymen alike. From his teacher, Rabbi Shakhna, he adopted the tendency to leave the ultimate decision in religious matters to the scholar to whom they were submitted, rather than spell them out in a definite form in the law books. He manifested his adherence to this principle by stating in the introduction to *Torath Hatath*: "It is not my intention to tell others to accept my viewpoint." This statement was frequently repeated in other works by equally forceful pronouncements, such as "all (decisions) depend on (the nature) of the problem," and "all (decisions) depend on the opinion of the rabbi." His purpose obviously was not to tie too tightly the hands of those who use his works as a guide to their religious life. This tendency to give flexibility to the law frightened his contemporaries and provoked sharp opposition. A schoolmate, Rabbi Hayim ben Bezalel, a brilliant thinker and writer, was afraid that freedom in rendering legal decisions together with the popularizing tendency of *Torath Hatath* and *Mappah,* would make it possible for unauthorized people to make decisions. His worries grew stronger when he became aware of how rapidly the use of *Torath Hatath* had spread. He therefore sharply censured Isserles for having failed to state clearly that only professionally trained rabbis might use the book.

It appears that Rabbi Moses was not very impressed by the arguments of his opponents. True, he was not by nature the humanist eager to attack his adversaries. But he was deeply convinced of the correctness of his approach and quietly disregarded the views of the opposition. Moreover, he often argued halakhic problems with ideas borrowed from the sciences, though this was rather uncommon among Poland's talmudic scholars. We have seen how he courageously performed a marriage ceremony on a Friday after sunset. That only few approved of this act is amply shown by the ordinance, decreed somewhat later by Cracow's Jewish communal leadership, which forbade marriages on Fridays. This prohibition, still valid after four hundred years, was enacted in order to prevent similar occurrences. Isserles' greatest innovation as a *possek,* however, were the concepts of *hefsed merubeh,* "considerable loss," and *sheath hadohak,* "time of emergency," which he applied very frequently in the Halakhah, and which he raised to the rank of all-important principles. According to these principles one should act with leniency in deciding religious questions in cases where a rigid interpretation of the law would result in grave financial loss; similarly leniency is advised in time of emergency. Most of the time Rabbi Moses applied these two principles in cases where the law was not specifically strict. Rabbi Hayim ben Bezalel, however, proved that in fact Isserles recommended leniency even with regard to cases where earlier authorities clearly ordered a strict application of the law. Isserles, of course, manifested real courage when he permitted himself to criticize and to correct the writings of Joseph Karo, who was an aged scholar of universally recognized authority. His contention that Joseph Karo "froze" the Halakhah in accordance with his own opinions was valid. Thus, wherever he found that the custom of Ashkenazic Jewry was different from Karo's decision, he wrote his comment into Karo's text and added the concluding remark "and so we (Ashkenazic Jews) act."

Rabbi Moses Isserles' determined defense of his halakhic attitudes on the one hand, and the gentle way in which he treated the opinions of his opponents on the other, is responsible for the difficulty one has in determining whether he was a *mekil*, lenient in interpreting the law, or a *mahamir*, a rigorous jurist. Some modern scholars point out that Isserles was a *mekil* only where leading medieval Ashkenazic jurists recommended a lenient interpretation. Other scholars, to the contrary, call attention to the fact that in such a vital area of Jewish law as the Sabbath, Moses Isserles manifested himself clearly as a *mekil*. They also indicate that Isserles' schoolmate and critic, Hayim ben Bezalel, contended that he was too much of a *mekil*, and that too often he freed the people from the "yoke" of a strict interpretation of the law. Rabbi Hayim ben Bezalel certainly went too far when he twisted the translation of the title of one of Rabbi Moses Isserles' works, *Torath Hatath, The Law of the Sin Offering,* into "Teaching of Sin," because, according to him, that book is a literary sin.

A proof that Moses Isserles in general was not a *mahamir* is the fact that he so often invoked the principles of "considerable loss" and "time of emergency." To be sure, there were Jewish legal authorities before him who applied these concepts in cases of emergency. But it was Moses Isserles who elevated them to principles of permanent validity. In addition, introducing them into the *Shulhan Arukh* through his *Mappah*, he established them as universally accepted. Nevertheless, these two concepts were not the central principle of Isserles' halakhic interpretations. The central idea that guided him and let him appear here as a *mekil* and there as a *mahamir* was his overwhelming loyalty to the *minhag Ashkenaz*, the religious practice customary in West European Jewry, and especially to the way in which it crystallized among the Jews of Poland. His teacher Rabbi Shakhna once made a decision which even contradicted the opinions of the Talmudic scholars of Germany, only because the local *minhag* of the city of Posen differed.

Isserles also had boundless reverence for the *minhag* because he believed the true soul of the people is revealed therein. One of his favorite statements was the Talmudic dictum "Go forth and see how the public are accustomed to act" (Berakhoth 45). Because he believed that it was man's duty not to accept things as authoritative, but rather to try to understand them, he often made an effort to discover the reason for a particular *minhag*. On the other hand, he never repealed a *minhag* just because its reason remained hidden to him. A scholar who has done extensive research in Isserles' writings thinks that in his *Darkhe Mosheh* the author accorded to the *minhag* the status of a *din,* a definite law. This is not to say that he tried to discover the hidden elements of a *din* in a *minhag*. He simply granted the *minhag* a validity equivalent to that of a law. It is certain that the starting point of Isserles' criticism of the *Shulhan Arukh* is the gap between the law as formulated by Rabbi Joseph Karo and the *minhag* of Poland. In his introduction to *Torath Hatath,* he states somewhat harshly that he who reaches religious decisions as formulated in the works of Rabbi Joseph Karo, especially in the area of the laws of "the forbidden and the permitted," acts in a manner contrary to all the customs that are practiced by Polish Jewry. In a similar vein he commented on the *Shulhan Arukh* in the introduction to the *Mappah*: ". . . and the Table (that is, the Prepared Table) is not yet the Table that he (Joseph Karo) had prepared for God, and he (Joseph Karo) had not given it yet to the people of these regions who practice their religious life mostly not according to his opinions." In order to correct all of this he wrote his works and became what he wanted to be—a teacher and a religious leader of Polish Jewry, of whom he was part and among whom he acquired his enormous Jewish knowledge.

The Jewish community of Poland paid homage to its great teacher during his lifetime and has done so until today. His works and his image as a religious leader of high stature entrenched themselves deeply within people's hearts. His critics were never able to weaken the position he won for himself. His sharpest opponent, Hayim ben Bezalel, relates that *Torath*

Hatath has become a widely used book and that it is considered the definitive manual of the laws of "the forbidden and the permitted." One of Isserles' pupils, Rabbi Benjamin Solnik, tells us with a somewhat enthusiastic exaggeration that his teacher's decisions have been accepted by all the Jewish people. Rabbi Isaiah Horowitz, a famed author who lived in the subsequent generation, asserts that Isserles' legal decisions were fully accepted in all the countries inhabited by Ashkenazic Jews. Isserles himself had a clear feeling that the *Shulhan Arukh,* together with his *Mappah,* became the most important Jewish code of laws. His greatest triumph, however, lies in the fact that Polish Jewry followed the Halakhah according to his formulations, even in cases where they were contrary to the opinions of Rabbi Solomon Luria, his contemporary, who was a more original halakhic thinker than he.

VI.

Rabbi Solomon Luria, known as Rashal or Maharshal, was somewhat older than Rabbi Moses Isserles. He, too, stemmed from a family that immigrated from Germany and traced its origins to Rashi, the famous French scholar of the eleventh century. We know neither the place nor the year of his birth. It is probable that he was born early in the sixteenth century, perhaps about 1510. There are some vague indications that he was born in Posen. At any rate, he spent his youth in Posen as a pupil of his maternal grandfather, a very pious and learned rabbi. As a young man Solomon went to the eastern part of the country and was, therefore, sometimes called Rabbi Solomon of Lithuania. In 1539 we find him in Brest Litovsk, one of the leading Lithuanian communities, where he probably served as a rabbi. He later became rabbi of Ostrog, an equally important community.

In Brest Litovsk, though only about thirty years old, his fame as a scholar was established. Questions in the area of religious law were frequently directed to him even from distant

countries. Wherever Rabbi Solomon stayed he opened a yeshivah. It seems that he excelled as a teacher, and pupils in the
hundreds flocked to him from "all the four corners of the
world." Reliable sources tell us that all the great scholars of
the epoch were at one time or another his pupils.

Rabbi Solomon was a man of firm character. Since he was
also an extremely honest and upright man, he had many conflicts with various people. Conflicts developed even between
him and his students. Late in his life Rabbi Solomon Luria
settled in Lublin. There is a likelihood that he was appointed
the first rector of the communal yeshivah that was opened in
1567 under a royal patent. It is possible that this was the
cause for his never-ending feuds with Israel, Rabbi Shakhna's
son, who was Lublin's communal rabbi at that time. Rabbi
Solomon Luria was a determined opponent of the Pilpul. It
was therefore obvious that tension would develop between
his school and the school founded by Rabbi Shakhna. Unfortunately, the conflict between the two methods of study caused
personal animosity between the heads of the schools. The
struggle reached the point where a number of Luria's students
left his school and entered the competing institution.

That some of the yeshivahs attracted many students because
of the financial backing given to them by the families of their
founders disturbed Rabbi Solomon. He was very outspoken
in this regard and deplored the fact that everybody coveted
the rabbinic degree. The much exaggerated criticisms he voiced
did not win him many friends. The continuous struggles naturally brought him many years of ever increasing hardship, dis-
illusionment, and sadness. He died a bitter man in Lublin in
November, 1573. Although he lived in Lublin only during the
last few years of his life, Rabbi Solomon Luria's name became
closely connected with the city. Lublin's oldest and largest
synagogue, possibly identical with that built in 1567 adjacent
to the yeshivah, is named *Maharshal Shul*. As the great Rabbi
of Lublin, Solomon Luria entered history.

The many difficulties that Rabbi Solomon Luria encountered
during his lifetime were an external reflection of what was oc-

curring in his stormy soul. He possessed an inquisitive and critical mind. He clearly recognized the great value of the writings of men like Maimonides and Abraham ibn Ezra. Much like the men of the Renaissance, he also evinced a deep interest in historical research. We will see later that his method of Talmudic research was strikingly similar to that employed by the humanists. Nevertheless, he sharply attacked both Maimonides and Abraham ibn Ezra. Declaring himself a decided opponent of philosophy, he showed genuine interest in Jewish mysticism. These different and often contradictory tendencies created a constant restlessness in his soul. In addition, his method of study was a tedious and slow process into which he invested enormous effort. He would sometimes work on a single halakhic problem for days or weeks in order to arrive at its final solution. It is no wonder that he occasionally felt quite depressed and doubted the feasibility of continuing his work. In one of these moments of despair his deeply religious and mystic nature rescued him and restored his fading strength. He narrates the event in cryptic language befitting such a wondrous phenomenon: "Once, at nighttime, I saw a lamp—the commandment, and a light—the Torah (comp. Proverbs 6:23), as if it had been told me from Heaven that power and courage had been given to me by the Heavenly Kingdom and that the gates of light were opened to me, saying: study the Torah, pass decisions on what is forbidden and what is permitted and give guidance; be strong as a lion and put down your thoughts in writing and bring them as a gift to the people." Rabbi Hayim Joseph David Azulai, the well-known scholar and traveler of the eighteenth century, interpreted this statement as relating a sort of a Hanukkah miracle: Rabbi Solomon Luria, when he studied at night, had on his table a small candle that miraculously burned for many hours, and this was to him a sign that God looked with favor on his work. The exalted language of the statement indicates, however, a much deeper religious experience, perhaps of the type of *gillui Eliahu* (Elijah's self-revelation), or the appearance of a *"maggid"* (familiar spirit). Such an experience was a true balsam to his restless, mystically inclined soul. It restored his courage and the will to continue his travails, which culminated in the composition of his works which count among the finest in Rabbinic literature.

When Rabbi Solomon Luria began to scrutinize all that had been written in the area of Rabbinic literature since the Sephardic sages began working on the codification of the mass of Jewish laws, he came to the conclusion that it was all unsatisfactory. He believed that most of these writings lacked clarity, and that a massive literature had grown up around the Talmud like a thick forest, so that the Talmud itself could not be seen anymore. True, Maimonides' code of laws was better and more clearly arranged than all other works of a similar nature. But Rabbi Solomon thought that Maimonides let himself be influenced too much by the philosophers and that he did not sufficiently take into consideration the opinions of the Tosafists. Though Maimonides was considered a saintly man and a scholar of towering stature by the Jewish people, Rabbi Solomon Luria did not hesitate to claim that the Tosafists, Rabbenu Tam and Rabbi Isaac the Elder, were his superiors as *posekim*, jurists. Luria further observed that the more the *posekim* discuss the various laws, the more contradictions develop among them. He therefore arrived at the drastic conclusion that the work of Rabbi Joseph Karo and Rabbi Moses Isserles was premature. He argued that before a definitively reliable work of the type of the *Shulkhan Arukh* could be written, the researcher should go back in the first place to the Talmud itself rather than acquire mere erudition in the writings of the *posekim*. Only in the Talmud can the *shoresh hainyan,* the "root of the matter" of each law be found. One should diligently search, he wrote, with all the seven methods of investigation (practiced in Jewish law) in order to discover the source and origin of each law. He believed that even this method of research would not lead to a total clarification of the laws because countless textual errors had crept into the Talmud over the course of the centuries before it began to be printed. Rabbenu Gershom, "the Light of the Exile," the great teacher of Western Jewry about the year one thousand, had already sternly censured those who would permit themselves to tamper with the text of the Talmud. About a century later, Rabbenu Tam resumed the fight against changes willfully introduced into the Talmud. He composed his *Sepher Hayashar* for the purpose of ridding the Talmud of erroneous texts. Now, after a period of four hundred years, numerous new errors had accumulated in the text of the Talmud. Rashi, the foremost commentary on the Talmud, and the work of the Tosafists were now also full of errors. The inherent danger in the textually inaccurate versions was heightened when the Talmud began to be printed, thus paving the way for the errors to become universally accepted. Luria therefore decided that his first goal in Jewish research should be to rid the text of the Talmud and of its foremost commentaries, Rashi and the Tosafists, of all their inaccuracies.

Rabbi Solomon Luria was a man who took everything very seriously. Hence the program of research that he undertook imposed a heavy burden of hard work upon him. He did not originally plan to write a special work for the purpose of "cleansing" the Talmud. He rather preferred to record his corrections on the margin of his own Talmud volumes as a sort of private research apparatus for his own exclusive use. In order to achieve the best possible results, he acquired old manuscripts of the Talmud and of other books that may have preserved the correct versions. The manuscripts were surely of help. The main result, however, was a product of his own clear reasoning and deep insight into the Talmud. Here and there he added a clarifying commentary to an obscure Talmudic passage. He arranged textual corrections of the commentaries of Rashi and the Tosafists on the Talmud in a similar fashion. All historians of Rabbinic literature agree that *Hokhmath Shelomoh, The Wisdom of Solomon,* the book in which this part of Luria's research has been collected, is a work of great originality and of major importance. The historian Heinrich Graetz correctly noticed the similarity between *Sepher Hayashar* of Rabbenu Tam and *Hokhmath Shelomoh,* and therefore called Luria the "Rabbenu Tam of the sixteenth century." The work reveals Rabbi Solomon Luria as a very able textual critic, who employed all the refined means of criticism current at that time and still used by modern scholars. It will be recalled that Luria did not intend to publish his critical notes on the Talmud. After his death, a thoughtful publisher acquired his private Talmud volumes from his sons and published the notes he found on the margins in book form. It was this publisher who gave the book the well-deserved name—*Hokhmath Shelomoh*. Many of Luria's corrections became so acceptable that later publishers of the Talmud amended the text in accordance with them. This made it possible, of course, to delete the material from later editions of *Hokhmath Shelomoh*. The book thus underwent a "shrinking" process. It is presently much smaller than it had originally been. This is the best proof of the greatness of the work.

Hokhmath Shelomoh was a tool that Solomon Luria prepared to facilitate his research. His *magnum opus*, however, is *Yam shel Shelomoh, The Sea of Solomon* (comp. I Kings 7:23–24). In this title we find the author's name as well as a symbol of the vastness and depth of the Talmud which is compared to that of a sea. Luria's ambition was to create in this work what Joseph Karo, according to him, did not succeed in accomplishing. His goal was to compose a work that would be the definitive handbook in which each and every Jewish law could be easily found. He sometimes even referred to his work as a "*Shulhan Arukh*," the name Rabbi Joseph Karo gave his own halakhic handbook. Rabbi Solomon Luria did not want to reach his goal by composing his work in a superficial manner. He did not want to walk in Maimonides' steps, who in his code did not quote the sources. Similarly, he did not accept Karo's method of considering only some of the early authors and ignoring the rest. He believed that before reaching a legal conclusion one is duty-bound to review all the opinions of former scholars and to analyze their Talmudic validity. Only then, he believed, is one entitled to consider his own opinion as binding. He also thought of writing his work in such a manner that it would simultaneously become the definitive com-

mentary to the Talmud and would make further work in this
direction superfluous.

Needless to say, by employing this method and setting before himself these goals, Rabbi Solomon Luria made his task
unmanageable and sentenced it to remain a torso. Strict adherence to the plan necessitated years of work on one single
tractate of the Talmud. Being extremely honest intellectually,
Rabbi Solomon Luria sometimes dwelt on a minor problem for
a full week until it became perfectly clear to him. He worked
on Yevamoth and Ketuboth, the tractates that discuss Jewish
marriage law, for three full years. Of the latter tractate, he
succeeded in writing a commentary for only two chapters. "I
searched," he tells us, "with the greatest effort of concentrated
thinking, with little sleep and much discussion with my colleagues, and even more with my pupils, and all my mind was
with the book. . . . "

By dint of hard labor and despite all difficulties, Rabbi Solomon Luria managed to write his commentary on almost all
the tractates of the Talmud that are primarily studied in the
yeshivahs and in adult-study groups. One of his pupils relates
that the master completed his commentary on not less than six-
teen tractates of the Talmud. His work was similar, observed
Isaiah Sonne, to the humanists' research in classical Latin literature. There is in *Yam shel Shlomoh* something of the culture
of the Renaissance. Though the work is not arranged in the
form of a code of laws, a very clear order is nevertheless discernible in it. Preceding each discourse is a short introduction
which briefly describes the law as it results from the discourse
proper. In other words, when the reader wanted simply to
know the law, he could easily find it. A student who desired
to penetrate the legal problem more thoroughly had at his
disposal an apparatus of all the relevant sources. Luria's
sources are richer and more varied than those of other contemporary rabbinic writers. *Yam shel Shelomoh* is indeed,
one of the finest works in the vast literature of Talmudic
exegesis, in which complicated matters are disentangled with
clarity. Luria, in addition, had a superior literary ability at his

command. His Hebrew style is much more beautiful and grammatically more correct than that of all his contemporaries in Poland. The excellent character of the work was a fact already known to his contemporaries. At the publication of the volume on Bava Kamma, the tractate that discusses Jewish civil law, the heads of the major Jewish communities in Poland, Austria, Bohemia, and Moravia took the unusual step of publicly recommending the book in the synagogues and urging scholars to acquire it. The recommendation was signed by the most famous scholars of the time.

The place that Rabbi Solomon Luria earned for himself in the literary history of the Jewish people is of the utmost importance. He insisted on thoroughness in the study of Jewish law and so created a literary work of a new type. In describing his own method of research, Luria states that he always made an effort to penetrate the depths of the Halakhah. In the hunt for abridged handbooks, about which Moses Isserles reports, and at a time when a tendency towards systematically codified legal literature was universal, Luria persistently reminded the scholarly world that the Talmud is and always will remain the major source of the Halakhah. About one hundred years after Rabbi Solomon's death, a group of young scholars in Kalisz was organized for the expressed purpose of studying Jewish law according to his advice: "Begin by examining the text of the Talmud carefully. Follow it up with an equally careful study of the Commentary of Rashi and of the critical notes of the Tosafists. Raising *kushioth,* questioning arguments, from one tractate of the Talmud to another should be avoided . . . ."

Rabbi Solomon Luria's preoccupation with Halakhah did not engross his total personality. We have seen that he evinced a lively interest in mysticism, and occasionally, though not too often, he introduced kabbalistic elements into his halakhic writings. In his spiritual life, however, prayer was of major significance. His responsa occasionally consider the prayer ritual. The warmth with which he treats the problem, and the many details about his own way of praying that he relates, convince us that he apprehended the worship of God as a deep religious experience and not only a matter of routine.

For his private use, he prepared a prayer book carefully corrected on the basis of old hand-written texts. His style of prayer and his religious practice in general are lovingly recorded in the eloquent *Matte Moshe, Moses' Rod,* by one of his brilliant students, Rabbi Moses of Przemysl. Rabbi Solomon Luria was also the greatest *paytan,* author of liturgic poems, among his contemporaries in Poland. He also regarded the study of the Pentateuch as an important matter. Characteristically, this interest was manifested at a time when the intellectual highbrows either did away with it altogether or treated it as a subject that did not require any real study. Luria, it seems, taught a daily class in the Pentateuch. The notes he wrote on the most popular commentary to the Pentateuch, that of his ancestor Rashi, probably grew out of this class.

Another of Luria's works of major importance is his volume of *Responsa,* published shortly after his death and republished several times later. Responsa are collections of questions in matters of Halakhah directed to a great jurist, together with his replies. The custom of submitting legal and religious problems to great rabbis in writing evolved during the early Middle Ages when the Jewish communities began to spread all over the world, farther and farther away from the center of Jewish learning in Iraq. The responsa quickly became a favored and widely used genre of Rabbinic literature. It is not surprising that when Rabbinic literature emerged in Poland, collections of responsa appeared there as well. Besides Luria's collection of responsa, Moses Isserles also left one. A third collection of responsa was *Sheerith Yoseph, The Remnant of Joseph* (comp. Amos 5:15), by Rabbi Joseph Katz, Isserles' brother-in-law. He was a respected judge and rosh yeshivah in Cracow for more than half a century. These three collections of responsa deal with questions directed to them from all over, even from distant lands. Perhaps more than anything, the Responsa literature manifests the great intellectual progress of sixteenth century Polish Jewry. It was a Jewish center that was spiritually and culturally independent. It also gradually became a center to which Jews of many lands could turn for religious guidance.

VII.

During the period described above, many more scholars attained fame in Polish Jewry. Rabbi Moses Isserles and Rabbi Solomon Luria, however, eclipsed all of them in learning, in the number of students that they trained, and in literary productivity. The epoch can rightly be named after them. They both were fully aware of the heights to which they had brought the literary and scholarly endeavors of their time. This awareness produced a close relationship between them and a friendship which lasted for many years. Luria was older than Isserles and as a scholar and thinker more original. The contemporaries knew it, and possibly Isserles himself was aware of it. Isserles knew, and readily admitted, that Luria's command of the Hebrew language was superior to his, as was his literary skill. A comparison of the prefaces to their various works reveals that Rabbi Moses Isserles liked to employ many literary devices. Rabbi Solomon Luria, instead, writes in a simple, forceful, meaningful style.

The impact of Rabbi Moses Isserles upon his contemporaries and upon later generations was incomparably greater than that of Rabbi Solomon Luria. Isserles was a man who was personally successful. During all the years of his mature life he occupied the post of rabbi of the capital city and was always held in high esteem by his pupils and by all the people. Luria, however, was driven from one community to another, perpetually in conflict with his colleagues and even with his students. In the area of the Halakhah, Isserles' teachings were accepted by Western Jewry even with regard to laws about which Luria differed. A modern scholar has well said that Rabbi Moses Isserles criticized Rabbi Joseph Karo's *Shulhan Arukh* in a gentle manner and "conquered" it. Rabbi Solomon Luria, instead, attacked it with all his might and lost. The key to this lies in the character of the two great men.

Moses Isserles was a kind person who always took the opinions of his fellowmen into consideration. In every situation he searched for the positive, for what was acceptable to all, for harmony. He did not reject the Sephardic *Shulhan Arukh* in a categorical and harsh manner. He "arrived at a compromise" with it, and made it acceptable to Polish Jewry. Rabbi Solomon Luria, instead, clung firmly to his own opinions and was not capable of tolerating a different attitude. This ultimately led to a break between him and Isserles. Isserles always held his older friend in high esteem and often acted humbly towards him. When Luria attacked him sharply for his philosophical interests, he accepted the criticism in good grace and tried to defend himself. He even calmly accepted Luria's justified but clearly insulting remarks about Isserles' imperfect Hebrew style. All this, however, was to no avail. Luria ultimately hurled against Isserles the same accusation with which he confronted most contemporary jurists: that he was superficial and did not adequately penetrate the legal problems which he discussed or interpreted. A rift in their lifelong friendship then became inevitable. Rabbi Moses Isserles always desired to create harmony between the teachings of the rabbis, the mystics, and the philosophers. Solomon Luria remained all of his life a rigid jurist, who, as far as society was concerned, recognized only the absolute authority of the law. His life was therefore full of hardship and bitterness. His last resort was the mystical, deeply religious flicker in his soul. In the face of all his fights and of the perpetual contrasts around him, this feeling was to him an undisputed treasure and a consolation to his stormy soul.

CHAPTER FIVE

THE GOLDEN AGE

I.

In the decades following the deaths of Rabbi Moses Isserles and Rabbi Solomon Luria, and in the first years of the seventeenth century, it became evident to what extent Poland had become an important center of Jewish culture. It was as if a giant wave of intellectualism encompassed the population. Torah learning, indeed, became universal.

Here and there warnings were sounded by spiritual leaders that a considerable number of Jews were poorly educated and were unable to study the Pentateuch or to understand the Hebrew prayers. One has the impression, however, that these were merely a warning against complacency. This is born out by a report originating at the turn of the century that even the butchers of Cracow were fine scholars. The true character of the epoch finds its expression in the repeated admonitions of Abraham Horovitz, a philosophically trained rabbi-author, that his sons should study Torah in the morning, and also at night before they retire. He wishes that during the hours of the day, too, they should tear themselves away from the hustle and bustle of business and devote some time to study. He even asks his sons to study in the synagogue while the cantor chants the prayers—so far went an intellectual's passion for study! One of the greatest scholars of the epoch, Rabbi Mordecai Yaffe, explicitly stated in the same spirit that the purpose of man's life is to study Torah. The profoundest preacher of the time, Rabbi Ephraim Lunchits, envisaged a Jewish society divided into three classes: the communal leaders, the scholars (for whom study is the only occupation), and a class of laymen whose activity in economic endeavor will be justified by the support they provide for the scholars.

In all this intellectual drive the study of the Talmud occupied a central position. Rabbi Mordecai Yaffe ventured a statement that scholars do not need to study the Scriptures, but should instead devote most of their time to the Talmud. Another writer enthusiastically promised that the study of the Talmud would hasten the coming of the Messiah. He, too, gave definite preference to the study of the Talmud. Most of the thinkers who permitted the study of secular disciplines (see Chapter 6) did so in the conviction that it would facilitate the understanding of the Halakhah. Even the preachers, whose primary purpose was to expound the ethical way of life, had to make concessions to the intellectualism of the age and to devote their sermons partly to Talmudic jurisprudence. The knowledge of the Talmud became so universal that it even penetrated the circles of the Karaites. If Isaac of Troki, the author of an excellent work of religious polemic, was indeed a Karaite, members of this group too attained a high degree of knowledge in the great work their faith rejected. The widespread interest in these studies was realized by the publishers of Hebrew books. About every fourth Hebrew book printed in Poland in that period deals with Talmudic and Halakhic subjects.

Most of the intellectual drive, and especially the concentration on the study of the Talmud, centered, as in the preceding period, in the circles of the Jewish aristocracy. These were the times when Poland's economy reached the peak of its expansion. Many Jews played an important role in the world of business. From their midst came most of the communal leaders, and a majority of them were Talmudic scholars. Some of the aristocrats belonged to the upper stratum of Jewish scholarship. Wealthy young men served as rabbis in smaller and larger communities. Their greatest ambition was to establish new yeshivahs in which they would be surrounded by alert students and where they could devote all their time and interest to the study of the Talmud. The poorer classes of Jewish society, captivated by the general intellectual drive, concentrated mainly on the establishment of societies for the purpose of study and of daily recitation of the Psalms.

The legal texts that were so eagerly studied were all in Hebrew and Aramaic. But the learned discussion, as long as it was oral, was conducted in Yiddish, the spoken language of the bulk of Polish Jewry. A manuscript survived with notes in Yiddish taken by a student of Rabbi Meir of Lublin. Obviously, the great scholar presented his lectures in Yiddish. However, when one had to commit his thoughts into writing, he usually did it in a "scholarly" Hebrew, in which numerous Aramaic idioms and quotations were organically intertwined with a Hebrew style that did not pay too much attention to the rules of grammar. There were, however, not infrequent cases of talmudically trained scholars who were incapable of producing their literary work in Hebrew. These people were often encouraged to write in Yiddish, the everyday language. A certain author, Abraham the Druggist, explicitly demands from the readers that they patronize literature in Yiddish in case they are not familiar with the holy tongue. He himself set an example by composing a bi-lingual, Hebrew-Yiddish ethical treatise. The considerable number of Yiddish books published in that period in Poland shows the eagerness of the people to read in Yiddish.

The use of the everyday language (Yiddish) spread more and more. True, the use of the Slavonic languages was still not uncommon, especially in the eastern regions of the sprawling country. However, the immigration in increasing numbers of Jews from Poland's West to the eastern and southeastern provinces established there also more firmly the use of Yiddish. The responsa literature, that often records testimony in its precise wording, contains many such texts in Yiddish. Rabbi Solomon Luria called the Yiddish language *leshon Ashkenaz gassah*, i.e., vernacular German. By this he probably meant to say that Yiddish was much different from the German language then in use in Germany. Yiddish, indeed, underwent in Poland in those times a process of "judaization," that is to say, it grew more and more distant from the language of the German Gentiles. To be sure, the Slavonic elements in Yiddish were not yet as numerous as they became in later generations. And yet Yiddish was now rapidly drawing away from its Middle High German roots. The burgesses of Poland's cities, who to a large extent stemmed from Germany and spoke German, began in those times to use the Polish tongue more frequently. Consequently, the Jews were less exposed to the German colloquial used by their neighbors, and their own Yiddish became more "Jewish." In this language they spoke and studied, and a Lithuanian rabbi, Meir Cohen, about the year 1600, expressed the wish that all the Jews of Poland would speak Yiddish. Then, he was convinced, all of them would be "full of knowledge." With this statement the rabbi, of course, wanted to give recognition to the fact that Jewish culture was brought to Poland mainly by the Yiddish-speaking immigrants from Germany. The only thinker who demanded that the people should speak Hebrew, especially on the Sabbath, was Rabbi Isaiah Horovitz, known as Shelah. This great kabbalist dreamed of a Jewish life full of holiness, and assigned to the holy tongue a role in the sanctification of the life of the Jew.

A further glimpse of the cultural life of the Jew in Poland reveals that its Renaissance character gained strength in these times. Immigrants from Italy settled both in Poland and in Lithuania. Here and there, as in Italy, we find a Jewish scholar who, in the manner of the humanists "criticizes the teachings of the rabbis." The intellectual drive as a whole, as it appears among the Jewish aristocracy, very much resembles trends in Italy's Jewish community in the Renaissance.

However, much as in Italy at the turn of the century, we notice also in Poland a longing for more genuine Jewish patterns of life. To Rabbi Abraham Horovitz, as we have seen, study meant so much that he advised his sons to study when the cantor chants the prayers in the synagogue. The sons, however, viewed the father's advice with reservations. Their generation had already developed a more pietistic outlook and tended to put prayer above study. A contemporary rabbi expressed his deep regret that for him "study was only a matter of routine, in order to acquire knowledge rather than to be careful in observing the *mitswoth*." Indeed, when the sixteenth century drew to its end, the Polish Jew was studying for the purpose of performing the *mitswah* of Torah learning; it was no longer a mere intellectual endeavor.

II.

During this period, Lithuania, the northeastern region of the Polish Commonwealth, began to play a more conspicuous part in the cultural life of Eastern European Jewry. The Duchy of Lithuania was generally a backward area in Poland. The great cultural upswing that the country experienced in the sixteenth century was little noticed there. An exception, however, was Lithuania's Jewish community. We have seen how in the fifteenth century it had close contacts with Kiev, whose Jewish community was a great cultural center. In the sixteenth century Lithuanian Jewry turned westward and increasingly became an integral part of Polish Jewry, especially after the Lublin Union (1569) welded Poland and Lithuania into a more organic unity. Jewish communities existed in many cities and towns. Some of them were large communities such as those of Brest-Litovsk, Grodno, and Pinsk.

The Jewish community in the capital city of Vilna, which later came to be known as *Jerusalem in Lithuania,* also began then to develop more rapidly. Vilna could not have harbored so many great scholars a generation later unless an intensive, formative, cultural activity had developed in the period now under discussion. A legend current among the Jews of Vilna clearly implied that Vilna's cultural growth was due to stimuli that came from Poland. According to this legend none other than Rabbi Moses Isserles sent Vilna its first great rabbi. A local historian contends that only because Vilna did not possess a Hebrew printing press, as did Cracow and Lublin, her scholars did not attain literary fame. Two leading Polish rabbis, the great Solomon Luria and Mordecai Yaffe, served as rabbis in other Lithuanian communities, the first in Brest-Litovsk and the second in Grodno. Another of Grodno's rabbis was a well-known scholar and author, Nathan Shapiro. Lithuania also had at that time her own yeshivahs. One of them, in Brest-Litovsk, became widely known and had among its students young men from the Crimea and from Italy. One of the students, Saul Wahl, was the son of the chief rabbi of Venice. He remained all his life in Brest-Litovsk and became widely known as a merchant-prince, communal leader, and magnanimous supporter of learning. A widely believed folk legend made him a king of Poland for one night.

III.

Of great importance was the increased activity of the printing presses in Cracow and Lublin. True, even now many books printed in other countries were sold in Poland. Booksellers continued to obtain governmental permission to import Jewish books from abroad. In 1580 a special agent came from Basle, Switzerland to sell the Talmud edition that was being published there. However, Poland's Jewish bookmarket in all probability distributed primarily books printed in Cracow and in Lublin. During the last three decades of the century more than two hundred books in various fields of Jewish literature were published by these local publishing houses. About one hundred and fifty of them were published by the printing press of Cracow, under the able and devoted management of Isaac of Prostitz. The Cracow press always employed excellent proof-readers, and by and large the texts published by it are of great accuracy.

The printing press of Lublin was at first not well organized, and the books it published showed poor craftsmanship. In 1570 the press acquired new type, its publications became more beautiful, and their prices increased considerably. The printers also began to prepare the manuscripts more carefully. When in

1574 they published the tractate Avoda Zarah, Strange Worship, Idolatry, they made great efforts to obtain old, reliable manuscripts. In 1580 the press closed down for a full decade, possibly because of competition from abroad. When it reopened in 1590, its work was again considerably improved and its publications were very beautiful.

The importance of local book production was generally recognized. People of means began to help financially in the publication of books. Proper recognition came also from scholarly circles. Rabbi Hayim ben Bezalel justly pointed out the connection between the printing of books and the spread of culture. Rabbi Eliezer Ashkenazi, an immigrant scholar and author, saw in the invention of the art of printing a special favor that God bestowed upon His people.

It is hard to estimate how many books the public acquired and how large the libraries were. We do not hear in Poland of that period complaints about a shortage of books, such as were common in Italy, where the papal authorities curtailed the publication of Hebrew books. But it seems that the distribution of books had not yet gained full momentum. Several rabbis mention their libraries in passing. The previously mentioned rabbi of Grodno, Nathan Shapiro, possessed a valuable library and many old manuscripts. Rabbi Joshua Falk, a leading rosh yeshivah in Lemberg, also had an important library. The greatest bibliophile known to us, however, seems to have been a scholar who neither attained the position of a rabbi nor that of a rosh yeshivah. David the Preacher, a remarkable personality, had collected books almost all his life. Though he was very far from being a rich man, he brought together, at a considerable expense, a valuable collection of more than 400 books. His ambition was to establish an institute of adult studies of which his library would ultimately become a part.

IV.

Once more the focal point of all cultural activities was the *yeshivah*. These schools continued to enjoy a high reputation

both in Poland and abroad. Students flocked to them from
distant regions. Two of the leading scholars of the epoch, Rabbi
Meir of Lublin and Rabbi Samuel Edels, always spoke highly
of the Polish yeshivahs. Whenever Meir spoke about the schools
that he directed in various cities, he described each of them as
"my great, high, and exalted yeshivah." Rabbi Samuel Edels,
in turn, was so convinced of the importance of group study in
the yeshivah that when he composed his genial commentary
on the Talmud, he excluded a part of tractate Sabbath from it
because he had never discussed it in the classroom. It was
pointed out above that young aristocratic scholars aspired to a
career of rosh yeshivah. The sources make it clear that a communal rabbi gained in prestige when he was given the additional position of a rosh yeshivah. In his responsa Rabbi Meir
of Lublin never fails to address his correspondents with the
title *rosh methivta,* head of the yeshivah. The high status in
Jewish society that a yeshivah enjoyed stimulated the establishment of many new schools of this type. The preacher Rabbi
Ephraim Lunchits reports in the introduction to his work *Orah
Lehayim, The Way of Life* (comp. Proverbs 10:17), that he
composed in 1595, that Poland is filled with yeshivahs. Also
Rabbi Meir of Lublin spoke of the "yeshivahs of all our
country." In the first line naturally stood the schools of the four
leading communities—Cracow, Lublin, Posen and Lemberg.
They all were headed by the communal rabbis, who, as we
shall see, were among the greatest scholars of the epoch. The
high esteem in which these schools were held by Jews in other
countries could be seen when in 1590 a terrible fire destroyed
the Jewish section of Posen with all its buildings and institutions. The rabbi of Frankfort, Akiba ben Jacob, who knew
the conditions in Posen's Jewish community well, composed
two poems in which he mourned the great calamity. "A city
full of Torah," he called Posen, and mourned bitterly the ruin
of its yeshivah, whose scholars were sharp of mind and great
in Pilpul. In the flowery fashion of the time he slightly
changed the name of the city to *Paz Naeh,* meaning in Hebrew
"as the finest gold beautiful." In this manner he wanted to

stress Posen's importance in the area of Torah learning and Jewish life.

Besides these well-established old schools, many are named that were hitherto unknown. The cities that are mentioned as locations of new yeshivahs were, no doubt, recorded accidentally and do not tell the full story of the yeshivah network. When one reads the sources one is impressed by the fact that many yeshivahs existed in the eastern and southeastern cities such as Brest-Litovsk, Pinsk, Grodno, Lutsk, Kovel, Przemysl, Belz, and Satanow. The most famous of the eastern yeshivahs, that of Ostrog, was surely one of the most important as it was headed by Rabbi Samuel Edels, one of the greatest scholars.

The establishment and support of a yeshivah was much like the maintenance of a modern university, a costly proposition. The salaries of the teaching personnel and the money that had to be spent for books and for the food and clothing of the students amounted to a large sum. Though the general impression is that the study of Torah on the yeshivah level was mostly pursued by young men from wealthy families, many students were recruited from the poorer strata of the population. An analysis of the sources from which the yeshivahs obtained their funds reveals that in most cases they were provided by magnanimous, wealthy individuals rather than by the organized *kehillah*. Polish Jewry in the late sixteenth century was a prosperous society that could run its institutions of learning on a voluntary basis. The financial support of the organized community therefore was not an absolute necessity. It was not until the beginning of the seventeenth century that the communities began to contribute considerably to the budgets of the yeshivahs.

Individual support of institutions of learning was in accord with the best tradition of the Renaissance. Christians also zealously supported higher learning. For the Jew, however, such support was a *mitswah*, a religious commandment. One of the great scholars of the epoch, a man with the strange name of Mosheh Meth, Moses the Dead (his friends liked to call him Moses the Living Man), asserted that "he who wants to be worthy of life in the hereafter, should care for the needs of yeshivah students and rabbis who study Torah for Heaven's sake," i.e.. those who do not occupy rabbinic positions. He even recommended that benefactors should help pay the salaries of the communal rabbis, so as to make sure that they would stay in the city permanently and make the study of Torah prosper. No wonder that we encounter manifestations of generosity of unusual dimensions. A few examples will suffice: The Italian born merchant-prince and legendary king Saul Wahl of Brest Litovsk had among his philanthropic ventures a private house of study. A group of scholars, fully cared for by him, carried on a constant "study vigil," so that the voice of Torah would never be stilled. A wealthy rabbi who died in Posen in 1597 left a large estate for the benefit of scholars. Seventeen years after the benefactor's death needy scholars were still supported by this fund. One is most impressed, however, by the manner in which Rabbi Isaiah Horovitz, author of the gigantic work *Shene Luhoth Haberith, The Two Tablets of the Covenant,* supported scholars. He spent the entire dowry that his bride received from her parents for this purpose.

These few illustrations are examples of pure philanthropy. The support of learning also took the form of the establishment of yeshivahs by wealthy individuals for the purpose of providing their learned relatives with positions of *rashe yeshivoth.* We have seen how Rabbi Solomon Luria expressed his dislike of this way of maintaining a school. And yet, at the turn of the century we again find some of the greatest scholars running such "family-established" yeshivahs. Israel Jozefowicz, a wealthy Jew of Lemberg, gave Rabbi Joshua Falk, the author of *Sefer Meirath Enayim, The Book that Enlightens the Eyes* (comp. Psalms 19:9), his well-educated daughter for a wife and established for him a yeshivah that he maintained a full quarter of a century. Of the same magnitude was the effort of Edel Ashkenazi of Posen who supported a yeshivah headed by her great son-in-law, Rabbi Samuel, known as *Maharsha,* for many years.

Less wealthy laymen, too, supported the study of Torah. They did so in a fashion popular down to the twentieth century—that is, by serving as hosts to needy students, each for a certain number of days. This custom ultimately became known as "eating days." In his bilingual ethical treatise *Sam Hayim, Life-Giving Drug* (a hint at the author's profession), Abraham the Druggist demands that the host should always be kind to his student-guest and should provide him with food even in times of economic depression. He advised the student to behave in a dignified manner at his host's table.

It goes without saying that the wealthier a yeshivah and the more famous its rosh yeshivah, the more students it attracted. It was the perpetual desire of the rashe yeshivoth to increase the number of their students. The prestige of a rosh yeshivah grew with every increase in the student body. In addition, the larger the student body, the greater the chance of its having a considerable number of *illuyim,* brilliant students, who were the pride of every academic institution. Rabbi Meir of Lublin's son says that each of the yeshivahs headed by his father (in Cracow, Lemberg, and Lublin), had an exceedingly large student body. This drive to attract masses of students to the yeshivahs also produced negative consequences. Rabbi Ephraim Lunchits claims that enthusiastic recruitment brought some young men to the yeshivoth who did not belong in that environment. This, no doubt, was the case in smaller schools which employed mediocre teachers. This situation was one of the reasons which prompted the communal leadership several decades later to establish a quota system for student admission determined by the size of the community.

Daily life in the yeshivahs will be thoroughly described in a later chapter. At this point, however, let it suffice to describe the yeshivah's "graduation requirements," although firm regulations were apparently never introduced. The training of rabbis was the primary practical purpose of the yeshivah. A student was ordained a rabbi when his teachers and "public opinion" among his fellow students agreed that he was duly versed in the law and qualified to make decisions in its various branches. This procedure, however, was not fully satisfactory. This becomes evident when one considers an action repeatedly taken by Rabbi Jehiel Michel Moravchik (died 1593). In his commentary on the Sayings of the Fathers named *Minhah Hadashah, New Offering* (comp. Numbers 28:26), published in 1577, he demanded that a young man should not be ordained "until he will be filled with the bread and wine of Torah," i.e., well versed in all branches of Jewish learning. His objections are repeated in another book *Seder Berakhoth, Order of the Blessings* (Cracow 1582). He explicitly demanded that yeshivah students should not be ordained before they reach the age of forty, as was customary in Italy. In addition, he wanted them to serve in the rabbinate for some time as assistants to older rabbis.

V.

The program of study in the yeshivahs did not undergo any noticeable changes after the death of Rabbi Moses Isserles and Rabbi Solomon Luria. Most of the rashe yeshivoth were their disciples and they continued to teach along the lines drawn by their masters. Now, too, time was divided between the study of the Gemara, with its commentaries Rashi and Tosafoth, the sources of the Halakhah, and the works of the medieval jurists, the applied Halakhah. We possess a somewhat idealized description of the program of studies that Nathan Hanover appended to his famous chronicle of the Great Catastrophe. Though this is a description of the yeshivahs of the middle of the seventeenth century, it is very likely that this program was already operative in the last decades of the sixteenth century. Hanover's description indicates that each semester was divided between two subjects: the first part of the semester was devoted to a discussion of texts from Gemara with Rashi and Tosafoth, and the second part to the study of the codes.

It is difficult to determine the reasons why both parts of the program were not studied daily, side by side. Hanover's description seems to indicate that this strange curriculum was introduced because of the perpetual wanderings of the students from yeshivah to yeshivah. The division of the term into two parts made it possible for the students to complete their courses in case they wished to transfer to another school in mid-term. To be sure, even when a student transferred to a new place during the part of the term when Gemara was studied, he did not miss much. The same tractate of the Talmud was studied simultaneously in all the yeshivahs. Torah study in the yeshivahs was, indeed, the great collective intellectual endeavor of Poland's entire Jewish community.

The study of Talmud in the yeshivahs was not confined to a simple explanation of the text. This type of instruction was offered to children in primary school (*heder*) at the age of six or seven. Advanced students, however, when entering a yeshivah, looked forward to the study of the Talmud with Tosafoth. The Tosafoth—short critical glosses to the Talmud—were the ideal basis from which one could easily ascend into the vastness of Pilpul. In those times "to study Gemara" usually meant to study Gemara with Tosafoth. Characteristically, the bilingual author Abraham the Druggist considered himself a non-educated Jew because he did not study Tosafoth and *halakhoth*. Nathan Hanover tells us that a *"halakhah"* stood for a full page of Gemara with Rashi and Tosafoth which each yeshivah student was expected to cover in a day of study. To be sure, Rabbi Isaiah Horovitz and Rabbi Levi ben Bezalel, who propagated far-reaching educational reforms, strongly emphasized the advisability of careful study of the text of the Gemara with Rashi in preparation for a pilpulistic analysis of the Tosafoth. The text of the Gemara, Isaiah Horovitz stressed, should be studied with diligence and with frequent repetitions.

The Pilpul, however, continued to blossom in the yeshivahs of Poland. It enjoyed the support of a host of adherents because of the intellectual interest it aroused among the students, and because—as it has been stated above in detail—it fitted the flamboyant personality of the Polish Jew so well. Adherents of the Pilpul now argued that the Pilpul was the surest criterion for evaluating the scholarship of a rosh yeshivah. They feared that the elimination of the Pilpul would make it possible for unqualified men to establish yeshivahs. They were of the opinion that if the ability to teach by this method were recognized as an absolute necessity, the ambitious drive of young, and perhaps immature, scholars to establish new yeshivahs would be checked.

Almost all leading scholars spoke out against this worship of the Pilpul, some mildly, others sharply. The Pilpul's most uncompromising opponents were Rabbi Isaiah Horovitz, Rabbi Levi ben Bezalel, and the energetic and outspoken preacher, Rabbi Ephraim Lunchits. In the introduction to *Orah Lehayim* Ephraim Lunchits described the faults of the Pilpul sarcastically and with derision. Levi ben Bezalel said in a fervent speech named *Derush al Hatorah, Sermon on the Torah,* and delivered in Posen on Shavuoth 1592, that the Pilpul should be called "stinging words" rather than "sharp thoughts." And Isaiah Horovitz deplored the fact that he devoted many years of his life to Pilpul, and implored the younger generation to avoid it.

Other scholars, too, saw the dangers inherent in this method of study. But they were not ready to eliminate it altogether. Even Isaiah Horovitz was of the opinion—much to our amazement—that "each one of us" is greater than the kabbalists of the Holy Land, because he is versed in the method of Pilpul, and even in the area of mystic lore one should employ "a deep and sweet pilpul." Rabbi Mordecai Yaffe voiced opposition only to the exaggerated use of the Pilpul, but believed that a "limited" application of the method would prove useful. Rabbi Moses the Dead wanted to see both methods of study in use. He suggested that a student should first study the text of the Talmud simply with the view of understanding it. A further step would be the re-study of the same text by means of the Pilpul. Rabbi Meir of Lublin was not generally in favor of Pilpul. But he could not deny that the Amoraim, the authors of the Gemara, sometimes employed this method. This fact compelled him, as well as Rabbi Levi ben Bezalel, to distinguish between the ancient Pilpul that was constructive, and the Pilpul of latter times which is, an empty Pilpul (*Pilpul shel hevel*). According to him, this sort of Pilpul diverts the student from truth and never leads him to his goal. Consequently, Rabbi Meir of Lublin confined the Pilpul to the yeshivah as a method of study, but eliminated it from his literary work.

The struggle against the Pilpul did not produce any visible results and the method continued to be employed in all its forms. Rabbi Levi ben Bezalel blamed the failure of his efforts on the fact that the scholars utilized the Pilpul as a lever in their professional careers. Rabbi Ephraim Lunchits writes that even scholars who in their hearts opposed the Pilpul, were not courageous enough to break with it openly because of its overwhelming popularity. Ultimately, even sermons primarily designed for the purpose of teaching a pious and ethical way of life had to resort to Pilpul in order to attract the audience. More than once a preacher would forget the primary purpose of his sermon and turn it into a display of sharp-minded, mental acrobatics. In a society of merchants, where sharp-mindedness and inventiveness were all-important and enjoyed the admiration of the scholars, the Pilpul could not simply be made to disappear. It was the most faithful and most eloquent expression of the mood of the epoch and of its people.

Since the study of Talmud was awarded the highest preference and the Pilpul was extolled by most of the people, the study of the legal codes was bound to suffer a partial setback. In addition, the two profoundest scholars of the epoch, Rabbi Meir of Lublin and Rabbi Samuel Edels, opposed this type of literature as a matter of principle. The study of the codes was still not altogether abandoned. The codes were assigned in the yeshivahs the second and shorter part of the semester. However, the necessity of training advisers in matters of the religious law made this study so imperative that the number of legal textbooks used in the schools even increased. Now, too, we find all the codes that were studied in the earlier period a basic part of the curriculum, i.e., *Mordecai, Rosh,* and *Arbaah Turim.* Also *Shaare Dura,* preferred by the students because of its conciseness, according to Isserles, retained its popularity. The rosh yeshivah of Grodno, Rabbi Nathan Shapiro, was repeatedly urged by his pupils to write a commentary to this textbook.

Rabbi Meir of Lublin wrote such a commentary. Rabbi Joshua Falk reports that he studied the above mentioned three codes with his associates and students. Commentaries on the *Mordecai* written then are sufficient in number to attest to the popularity of this code also.

Several new textbooks were added during this period to the yeshivah student's library. More use began to be made of two legal works of Sephardic origin, the *Halakhoth* of Rabbi Isaac Alfasi (died in 1103), a sort of abridgement of the Talmud, and the commentary of Rabbi Nissim Gerondi (fourteenth century) on Alfasi's work. These two works became more popular in the Ashkenazic communities as a result of the wide popularity of Rabbi Joseph Karo's *Beth Yosef,* the great repository of the Sephardic *halakhah.*

Also one of the best law collections of Ashkenazic origin, the *Sefer Mitswoth Gadol (The Great Book of Precepts)* by Rabbi Moses of Coucy in France, was used in the yeshivahs. This thirteenth-century writer was more than a talented rabbinic author. He was a great religious dreamer who undertook unusual preaching journeys with the purpose of bringing Jews closer to God. Several commentaries on this book were written in Poland during this period. Rabbi Abraham Horovitz, the philosopher-father of Rabbi Isaiah Horovitz, enthusiastically recommended Moses' work to his students. He considered it one of the best textbooks. About the same time, Rabbi Mordecai Yaffe composed the *Levushim, Raiments,* as a textbook for the yeshivahs. We will later have an opportunity to become more closely acquainted with this work.

VI.

The determining factor in the existence of a yeshivah, and the one upon which its prestige largely depended, was the personality of the rosh yeshivah. We have seen that when a rosh yeshivah belonged to a wealthy family that could support the institution, and especially the needs of the students, the school grew rapidly. It was a happy coincidence that at the turn of the century some of the greatest rashe yeshivoth possessed the two qualities of *Torah ugedulah*, i.e., were "supreme both in Torah and in worldly affairs" (Tractate *Gittin* 59a). Rabbi Mordecai Yafeh, a son of the magnate Abraham Judeus Bohemus, Rabbi Joshua Falk, Rabbi Samuel Edels, and Rabbi Isaiah Horovitz—all had abundant funds at their disposal for the maintenance of their yeshivahs. Wealth, however, was not the only means of attracting students. That the fame of the rosh yeshivah as a scholar was no less a determining factor is manifested by the huge numbers of students that Rabbi Meir of Lublin had in all his yeshivahs, and who were not, it seems, financially supported by his family. Further evidence is offered by the fact that the above-mentioned rashe yeshivoth were not only among the wealthy, but also among the greatest rabbinic authors of their time.

The social status of the rosh yeshivah was very high. It often surpassed that of the communal rabbi. The title preferred by the scholars in their learned correspondence was *resh methivta*, the Aramaic term for rosh yeshivah rather than *av beth din*, "head of the court," the title used by the communal rabbis. In smaller communities the same man usually held both positions. Large communities, with more than one yeshivah, had, of course, several rashe yeshivoth. Only one of them, however, held the additional position of the communal rabbi. The combined positions of rosh yeshivah and communal rabbi were, of course, the acme of a Polish Talmudic scholar's career. On the other hand, there were scholars, like Rabbi Joshua Falk, who purposely renounced the career of a communal rabbi in order to devote themselves solely to study and research as rashe yeshivoth and rabbinic writers. No doubt, they were only a handful.

Nathan Hanover, the seventeenth century writer, provided us with detailed information about the activities of the rosh yeshivah. A rosh yeshivah was the recognized leader of the scholars in every locality, and supervised Jewish elementary and secondary education. His main duty, however, was to at-

tend to the needs of the yeshivah. His daily lecture in the fore-
noon was the climax of the day in the yeshivah. This was true
not only of the first part of the term, when the theoretical
halakhah was studied, but also of the second part devoted to
the study of the codes. The rosh yeshivah gave much of his
time to the needs of the students. Rabbi Meir of Lublin very
much enjoyed writing extensive responsa to his colleagues.
But at the beginning of the school term, when he was busy with
the needs of the students, he drastically curtailed the time devoted to this preferred activity. We have seen that Rabbi Isaiah
Horovitz used his wife's dowry to support his pupils. And
when he sent the manuscript of his main work from the Holy
Land to his sons in Prague, he admonished them to always
permit young students to copy it for the purpose of study.

The high status of the rosh yeshivah and of the scholar in
general created a tendency in the community to care for their
economic well-being. After all, not all the rashe yeshivoth and
rabbis were sons or sons-in-law of the wealthy. Rabbi Solomon Luria had already clearly defined the duty of the community to care for its scholars: "especially (a scholar who)
teaches in a yeshivah may be supported from public funds."
In his work *Matte Moshe,* Rabbi Moses the Dead collected all
of the numerous references from the Talmud and from Rabbinic
literature pertaining to the custom of exempting scholars from
paying taxes. The class of the scholars was obviously numerous
and the problem of their economic interests was on the agenda.

The high status of the rashe yeshivoth, and especially of those
who also held the position of communal rabbis, evoked much
jealousy. Quarrels about rabbinic positions were not infrequent.
The conflicts were often aggravated by the fact that besides the
professional rabbis each community also had a considerable number of non-professional scholars. In these circles, and especially
among the wealthy of them, some people were reluctant to accept
fully the authority of the official rabbi. Much jealousy prevailed
also among the rashe yeshivoth themselves in their ambitious drive
to realize great personal careers. These phenomena were quite
frequent, and were evidently an inevitable part of the intellectual

drive of those times. The great preacher Rabbi Ephraim Lunchits bitterly deplored the lack of friendship and the presence of jealousy among his contemporaries. In this he saw the main reason for the failure of the spiritual leadership to act effectively against the shortcomings of the generation.

VII.

We have seen that each community had a number of non-professional scholars. These groups created nuclei of Torah study unaffiliated with yeshivahs. Nevertheless, it was occasionally claimed that these men were devoted solely to their economic endeavor and neglected study altogether. Rabbi Solomon Luria's pupil, who lived in the city of Miedzyrzec, asserted that no more than ten per cent of the learned laymen continued their studies.

These complaints, however, were, as pointed out above, directed against complacency, with the usual exaggeration of the propagandist. Most of the sources show that the problem of adult study was constantly under discussion. Certain writers gave advice about the time that is most suitable for study. Most of them agreed that it is best to study at night, but also demanded that some part of the day be devoted to the same purpose. Rabbi Moses the Dead demanded that the wealthy study during the day, since they usually are not very busy. In his above-mentioned work he reprinted a prayer for success in study that he found in an old book. The detailed instructions about study which Rabbi Abraham Horovitz gave to his sons were mentioned above. His son Rabbi Isaiah, the moralist, went even further and instructed his sons that when they build their homes, the plans should provide for special rooms in which "one could be alone to study and to repent." This great enthusiast hoped that his children would devote their entire lives to the study of Torah and to God's service.

The text mostly studied by learned laymen seems to have been the Mishnah. Many of them could no doubt have studied on a higher level of the Talmud with the Tosafoth in which they were trained in their youth at the yeshivahs. The study of Mishnah was, however, more suitable for them as it demanded less time and concentration. This explains the fact that a certain scholar, Joseph of Zaslav, specifically asked his sons to study the Mishnah. This may well be why Rabbi Levi ben Bezalel so energetically promoted the organization of societies for the study of Mishnah. To be sure, the sources tell us solely about his efforts in Bohemia with regard to this project. There is every reason to assume that he was similarly active during the two periods he served as rabbi of Posen. From his own reports, we know that his efforts to institute reforms in Torah study were also conducted in Poland. Rabbi Isaiah Horovitz went further. He recommended that the Mishnah be learned by heart, and pointed out in the manner of a kabbalist that in Hebrew the word "Mishnah" is composed of the same letters as the word *neshamah,* "soul." In other words, the study of the Mishnah is as essential to a Jew as the soul. Being a religious enthusiast, Rabbi Isaiah Horovitz was not satisfied to see his sons study the Mishnah alone. He demanded that they study the Talmud and the codes, and above all devote some of their time to the discipline which he considered the crown of all knowledge—the kabbalah.

A perusal of the sources gives the general impression that before the year 1600 Torah study outside of the yeshivahs was generally practiced on an individual basis. But the first signs of organized activity soon began to appear. For the time being, this organized activity, to be sure, resulted from the initiative of individuals, truly in the manner of the Renaissance. Such an initiative originated with Saul Wahl, the wealthy immigrant merchant and philanthropist. From his Italian homeland he knew the custom of establishing "private" academies in which lay scholars could congregate for the purpose of study and discussion. Such an academy, called in Hebrew *midrash,* was usually placed under the direction of a great scholar, whose support by the founder was in the tradition of the Italian Renaissance. When Saul became a wealthy and influential member of the Jewish community of Brest Litovsk, he established there such an "Italian" *midrash* under the supervision of a permanent rosh yeshivah. In order to secure a firm fiscal basis for the institution, Saul built a shopping center and endowed the academy with its proceeds. The academy was housed in a building which he especially erected for this purpose. In time this *midrash* became an important center of learning in Brest Litovsk.

Somewhat earlier, however, probably in 1571, a poor preacher made an effort to establish a *midrash* with a much wider scope. He wanted to start a new type of institution of learning that was almost completely unknown in Poland. The planner, David the Preacher, was a remarkable personality. He was born in Cracow in the 1520's. As a lad, he lived in Posen enjoying the support of a wealthy man. He was obviously born into a poor family. He relates that he was a student of Rabbi Moses Isserles and of Rabbi Solomon Luria. He, indeed, became a very fine scholar. We have seen that David was a great bibliophile. He began building his library at the age of nineteen, and in the course of a quarter of a century he assembled a valuable collection of more than four hundred volumes.

David the Preacher, it seems, never held a permanent position as communal rabbi or rosh-yeshivah. This was so, probably, because he was not promoted by any of the aristocratic families which controlled the communities. Consequently, he entered the profession of preacher to which many of the "proletarians" among the learned intelligentsia flocked. He was most probably a free-lance preacher. He travelled extensively, and we also find him in Moravia and in Italy. In the years 1556–1558, David was active in various cities in northern Italy. For a certain time he was in charge of a *midrash* established by a wealthy family in Ferrara. He later returned to Poland and was a successful and popular preacher in Cracow. David was very proud of his abilities as a preacher and expressed his feelings of gratitude to God for having granted him the *leshon limmudim*, the style of the speakers (comp. Isaiah 50:4 and

David Kimhi's commentary on this verse). The preachers used this term to describe their specific talent.

David the Preacher was also a brilliant writer. He wrote in a vivid and colorful Hebrew style, almost without grammatical errors; he also wrote Aramaic with ease. It was very easy for him to compose rhymed prose. In his letters, he appears to have possessed all of the literary skills of a Renaissance writer with the ability to exalt a friend and to destroy an enemy. David wrote a number of books, such as a collection of sermons on the Pentateuch, responsa, a guide for letter writing, and a popular textbook to help one memorize the 613 precepts of the Jewish religion. Being always very poor, he was unable to publish his books. He therefore printed in Cracow, in 1571, a pamphlet entitled *Shir Hamaaloth Ledavid, A Song of Ascents of David* (comp. Psalms 122:1), in which he published samples of his works with the hope that they would impress some maecenas who would then sponsor their complete publication. His expectations were not fulfilled. Earlier, in 1568, David published another small booklet entitled *Ketav Hitnatzluth Ladarshanim, An Epistle in Defense of the Preachers,* in which he made an eloquent effort to defend the preachers against the derision which society heaped upon them.

The sources at our disposal provide some data concerning the activities of this remarkable man. In 1568 David was dreaming about going to the Holy Land and devoting most of his time to literary activity. It seems that the plan did not materialize. In 1571, already in his forties, we find him in Cracow, very depressed and worried about the future of his unmarried daughters. He was ready to start a new journey, this time for the purpose of collecting dowries for the daughters. During these hardest days of his life, the eternal wanderer began to dream about finally settling in some town where he could live quietly amidst his books and studies. It was then that he conceived the plan of establishing somewhere in Poland a *midrash,* probably similar to the institution in Ferrara that was under his direction. The proletarian scholar was so captivated by his dream that he saw in it "the ultimate goal of everything."

The most valuable asset that David the Preacher was ready to put at the disposal of the new academy was his library, probably the only thing he possessed. According to the plan, the library was to be available for the use of the scholars. David was even prepared to lend the books for home study to those who were too tired to visit the academy in the evenings, after a day's activities in business. He planned to make the academy a center for veteran scholars, where they would be able to pursue learned discussions, and through his mediations, start a learned correspondence with scholars in other localities. He was also ready to forward questions in matters of law to the leading rabbis in the country. Another service of utmost importance that David's *midrash* was ready to give the public was instruction in Hebrew grammar to the teachers of the elementary schools (*melamdim*). He was convinced that this would be "a wonderful service to their young pupils." And finally he was prepared to give a daily popular lecture in Bible and in the ritual law to the public at large. This course, he was convinced, would be of great service especially to the poor people.

After elaborating his plan, David made a statement that he did not seek an official rabbinic position for himself or any other honors in the community which would agree to harbor his academy. From the beginning, he was ready to place himself in a status lower than that of the local rosh yeshivah. He was obviously worried lest the *rashe yeshivoth* oppose his plan. The *midrash* was, after all, a new type of institution hitherto almost unknown in Poland. By publishing the *Shir Hamaaloth Ledavid* he intended not only to find a publisher for his works but to show, he says, that he was qualified to head an institution of learning. In the closing statement of his plan, he could not abstain—true man of the Renaissance that he was—from extending a blessing to all those who would support his plan and a . . . curse upon its prospective opponents. We do not know whether David's plan ever materialized, and if it did, how long the *midrash* existed. But the plan is one of the remarkable phenomena in the area of adult studies in this period of a universal drive for learning.

The lay scholars, though a numerous group, were of course, a minority. Besides them there was the multitude of small retailers and craftsmen, who were never in a position to continue their studies beyond the elementary school (*heder*). Children of the lower strata of the population had in most cases to work as teenagers. But in the drive to study, both as an intellectual occupation and as the fulfillment of a great *mitswah,* they, too, could not remain excluded from the world of study. This type of Torah student became more conspicuous in a later period. But already then—the Maharam of Lublin reports—groups emerged for the purpose of reciting the Psalms every morning in an organized manner. It is also safe to assume that at least some members of the constantly spreading societies for the study of Mishnah came from these circles.

Yiddish literature played a decisive role in the education of this type of Jew whose knowledge of Hebrew and Aramaic, the languages of ancient Jewish literature, was hardly sufficient. The numerous Yiddish publications that flowed from the Hebrew printing press in Cracow indicate the measure in which Yiddish literature was culturally essential. We shall later examine this literature.

VIII.

The preachers (*darshanim*) made the greatest contribution to adult education. Some of them were great personalities in the full sense of this word. Besides them there was a host of preachers whose names are unknown to posterity. The preachers were mostly men of learning who in addition were endowed with the gift of oratory, but who for some reason could not obtain the position of a communal rabbi or rosh yeshivah. This, as we have seen, transformed them into a sort of "proletariat" within the scholarly community. The rabbis and the rashe yeshivoth generally felt secure in their positions, and were

not very dependent upon the public. The preacher, instead, had
to rely completely upon the masses. If he became popular, he
was honored and supported. But if he did not succeed in
gaining public acclaim, he remained without any social status
and without means of sustenance.

His dependence upon the masses made the preacher a controversial personality. The people demanded that a sermon
should be presented in an esthetic manner which would provide
enjoyment. In a society which worshipped the Pilpul, a
preacher, too, was expected to express keen thoughts, and—as
Rabbi Mordecai Yaffe narrates—to present "something new."
Requests of this type made the preacher primarily concerned
with the esthetic and intellectual aspects of the sermon, and in
this pursuit its main objective—to teach the masses Torah and
to encourage them in the practice of the precepts—was often
lost. The king of the preachers, Rabbi Ephraim Lunchits, relates that occasionally as soon as a preacher began to speak
about repentance and call the people to improve their social
behavior, the audience would stop him. Some lay scholars
went so far as to use their knowledge to show that everything
in Jewish society was perfect and that there was no need for
reproach.

Everybody, therefore, was somewhat unhappy with the
preachers. No less a spiritual leader than Rabbi Samuel Edels
criticized them and blamed them for not having sufficiently
penetrated the treasures stored in the Aggadah. Others contended that the preachers were not sufficiently learned and that
they were trying to cover up their ignorance with beautiful
phrases. They were blamed for permitting themselves too much
freedom in the "interpretation" of biblical passages. Finally,
they were accused of being primarily concerned with remuneration for the sermon rather than attending to their task of leading
the people in the paths of righteousness. This controversy induced some of the religious leaders to discuss the purpose of
the sermon. Their idea, it seems, was that the sermon should
address itself primarily to the poorly educated masses. Rabbi
Isaiah Horovitz and Rabbi Ephraim Lunchits both thought

the preacher should teach the weekly portion of the Scriptures (*sidrah*), some of the ritual laws, and provide moral instruction. Jehiel Michel Moravchik, a popular author, explicitly asked the preachers to translate every Hebrew word into Yiddish and not to take it for granted that their audiences understood the biblical passages they discussed. Rabbi Mordecai Yaffe recommended a more general goal to the preachers, namely, to help man to achieve ultimate perfection. The great rabbi brought this Renaissance ideal from Italy where he had lived a number of years.

How did the preachers react to the opposition they encountered so often? To begin with, they were proud of their dual talents: scholarship and oratory. In 1571, though besieged by worries and exhausted from his many peregrinations, David the Preacher thanked God for having bestowed upon him the talents of a preacher. Despite the harsh criticism, the preacher was much sought after. The demand that the masses should have a chance to hear a preacher every Sabbath was continually reiterated. They were, of course, also needed—as Mordecai Yaffe tells us—at every type of religious celebration, such as a wedding, a circumcision, and the like. The preachers had, after all, made a sincere effort to do justice to their task of calling the people to repentance. They did it, as pointed out above, by employing the *leshon limmudim,* the idiom of the speaker. That is to say, they would weave moral ideas into the fabric of their learned discussions, and thus implant them into the hearts of the audience. Because they addressed the people in Yiddish and in a popular manner, they usually achieved the goal of influencing the people. The preachers' pride in their maligned and controversial profession was manifested with much dignity in David the Preacher's above-mentioned *Epistle in Defense of the Preachers,* in which he demonstrated the importance of the sermon and discussed homiletical methodology.

The preachers' activities stimulated the emergence of a sermon literature. An index, *Imre Shefer, Goodly Words* (comp. Genesis 49:21. The reference to the title of the book and to the name of the author in this verse is obvious) by Rabbi Naphtali Altschuler was published, that listed sources in ancient Jewish literature where sermonic material could be found.

Also at that time one of the most important commentaries on the *Midrash Rabbah*, the classical *midrash* on the Pentateuch and on the Five Scrolls, was written in Poland. Its author was Rabbi Issachar Berman Hocohen of Szczebrzeszyn, Rabbi Manoah Hendel's a relative. He names his work *Matenoth Kehunah, Priestly Endowments* (comp. Bava Kamma 110G), certainly in order to stress his membership in a priestly family. Issachar Berman composed his commentary on the model of Rashi's commentary on the Torah. He made it his task to explain in simple words and in very short sentences various passages of the *midrash* so as to make it possible for the average man to study this classic with pleasure and without difficulties. The author approached his task armed with an enormous load of material collected from the Talmud and Biblical exegetical literature. He made ample use of grammatical material and of various Hebrew dictionaries. He introduced scientific data, in which he was quite at home, into his work. Like his contemporaries, he made painstaking efforts to establish the correct text of the *Midrash Rabbah*. This he achieved by using various old manuscripts. These efforts made the *Matenoth Kehunah* into a very fine commentary on the *midrash*. The book was first published in Cracow in 1597, and no doubt helped greatly to popularize the study of the *midrashim* in Poland, and stimulated interest in homiletical literature. The commentary has been re-published frequently down to our own times in a somewhat abridged form in the standard editions of the *Midrash Rabbah*.

A most remarkable phenomenon in this area, however, is the fact that Rabbi Samuel Edels, the greatest talmudic writer of the epoch, besides his *Hiddushe Halakhoth*, the commentary on the halakhic parts of the Talmud, also wrote the *Hiddushe Aggadoth*, a commentary on its aggadic parts. The great jurist was of the opinion that the Talmudic Aggadah is a great storehouse of the thoughts of the sages and that these should be utilized for the moral education of the people. Some historians believe that the *Hiddushe Aggadoth* represents a greater literary accomplishment than the *Hiddushe Halakhoth*.

Besides these works, which serve as raw material for the preacher, collections of finished sermons were written. Most of them were probably delivered orally originally and then converted into essays. A number of such homiletical collections was published in Cracow and in Lublin in the last decades of the century. Mordecai Yaffe complained that he did not have the necessary funds to publish a large collection of sermons "that I have preached," he says, "before large crowds." The volume *Levush Simhah Wesason, The Raiments of Gladness* and Joy (comp. Esther 8:16), that contains these sermons, is indeed, the only part of his great work *Raiments* that was never printed. The author of the famous Yiddish book Tseenah Ureenah wrote *Melits Yosher,* Preacher of Justice, (comp. Job 33:23), also in Yiddish, a collection of simple explanations of the Pentateuch. He intended this book for people who found it difficult to follow the dynamic presentation of an eloquent preacher, or who did not have a chance to hear one. This book of the extremely popular author remained almost unknown. A printed discourse could not match the living word, especially when presented by a talented preacher.

The greatest of the preachers of this epoch was the frequently mentioned Rabbi Ephraim Lunchits. His greatness as a preacher was fully matched in the literary field by his collections of sermons. Ephraim was born in the middle of the sixteenth century and was a disciple of Rabbi Solomon Luria. He was one of the eminent scholars of his times. His works show great erudition in the Bible, the Talmud, in medieval Jewish philosophy, and in many other areas of Jewish literature. He was especially outstanding, however, as a preacher. It seems that at the beginning he did not fare any better than his fellow-preachers. He, too, probably did not have a steady position and was an itinerant preacher. He later became so widely acclaimed as an excellent orator and an animated preacher that the Council of the Four Provinces invited him to preach at its sessions before the assembled rabbinic and lay leadership of Polish Jewry. It is worth noting that in the same period the great Catholic preacher, Piotr Skarga, delivered similar sermons at the sessions of the Polish Diet, calling attention to the ills of Polish society. Rabbi Ephraim's courageous preaching and his enduring struggle for the poor and weak made him many enemies in influential circles. He was nevertheless appointed a rosh yeshivah in Lemberg, though at a rather advanced age. He also became the first author to have a book published with the financial assistance of the Council of the Four Provinces. His *Keli Yakar, A Precious Instrument,* has become one of the most popular commentaries on the Pentateuch. He composed this work in 1601 in gratitude for recovering from a grave illness. Rabbi Ephraim ultimately gained full recognition when he was appointed in 1604 to the combined position of rabbi and rosh yeshivah in Prague. He remained in this leading position until his death in 1619.

Rabbi Ephraim's excellence as a preacher is clearly reflected in his writings. The living word of the sermon survived in his books much more than in the writings of other preacher-authors. His style is vivid, colorful, and laden with passion. At the same time, his thoughts are genuine and deeply anchored in the social and cultural challenges of the age. Like all the preachers he, too, interpreted biblical verses and rabbinic statements in an artistic and artificial manner in an effort to express a challenging thought. But his sincere passion for justice and the courage to reveal his thoughts detracted from the artificiality of his "sermonic frills." In his burning urge to preach the ethical way of life, the secret of his influence on later generations is hidden. Even his own contemporaries, who refused to listen to any preacher who too openly exposed the evils of the generation, gave heed to his exhortations. Ephraim was the only preacher in Ashkenazic Jewry who could be compared, in the beauty of his sermons, to the great Italian Jewish preachers of the Renaissance.

The unique position as a preacher that Rabbi Ephraim Lunchits occupies in Jewish cultural history is matched by his accomplishments as an author. Of his seven works, six were published in his lifetime. Few contemporary authors gained equal recognition. Almost all of his works were later re-published again and again, especially the *Keli Yakar* and *Oleloth Ephraim, The Gleanings of Ephraim* (comp. Judges 8:2). *The Oleloth Ephraim,* among all of his works, reflects his great talent best. This work, as well as *Orah Lehayim, Guide to Life* (comp. Proverbs 10:17), and *Ammude Shesh, Pillars of Marble,* contain sermons of perfect artistic accomplishment. The other three, *Ir Gibborim, City of the Mighty* (comp. Proverbs 21:22), his earliest work, *Keli Yakar,* and *Sifthe Daath, Lips of Knowledge* (comp. Malachi 2:7), present "raw material" for sermons. His seventh work, *Rivevoth Ephraim* (comp. Deuteronomy 33:17), was so voluminous that the author could not find the means to publish it.

The versatility of Ephraim's personality is reflected in his books. In one of the works he reveals himself a master of style; in another, the social reformer in him finds full expression. A third work puts him into focus as a great biblical commentator; and still another one—his first book—presents him as a communal leader. It is this abundance of talent, coupled with his passion for justice, that so deeply impressed his contemporaries and still moves his readers today.

Rabbi Isaiah Horovitz was a passionate preacher, full of unusual enthusiasm for Jewishness and justice. He was the author of the famous work *Sheney Luhoth Haberith, The Two Tables of the Covenant* (comp. Deuteronomy 9:15). He was a son of Abraham Horovitz, the philosophically trained rabbi mentioned above. Isaiah was born in the 1560's and studied under several great teachers, such as Rabbi Meir of Lublin, Rabbi Joshua Falk, and his own father. At a very early age, he was considered an important rabbi. In 1590, when he was not yet thirty, he was invited to join Poland's leading rabbis and sign a document of the greatest importance issued by the Council of the Four Provinces. During the last fifteen years of the century, Isaiah occupied various positions as a rabbi and rosh yeshivah in Poland. We have seen that he spent his wife's dowry for the maintenance of his students. He was an unusually charitable man. It may even be safe to assume that there is no exaggeration in his son's assertion that the father always had at his table no less than eighty poor guests. The son also tells us of his father's activities as a *darshan*: "He was a great preacher (and preached) with wondrous enthusiasm, and persuaded many people to abandon sin."

After Rabbi Isaiah Horovitz had spent the first part of his life in Poland, he left the country early in the seventeenth century to occupy rabbinic positions in leading communities in other lands, such as Frankfort, Metz, and Prague. His last years were spent in the Holy Land for the purpose of studying the mystic teachings of the Kabbalah in the saintly atmosphere of Jerusalem, Safed, and Tiberias. There he was persecuted by the Turkish governor. He was, nevertheless, able to conclude the composition of his giant work which he had begun to write while still living in Prague. He sent the manuscript to his sons in Europe, and passed away in Tiberias in the year 1630.

It is no easy task to describe the contents and the character of Rabbi Isaiah Horovitz' main work. It is a very large book, quantitatively possibly the largest that an East European Jewish scholar wrote in those times. This, and the unusual popularity of the book, necessitated an abridged edition. The book is written in a beautiful, fluent, exalted Hebrew style as if it were one great, long enthusiastic sermon, filling the heart of the reader with love of God and saintliness. One doubts whether Jewish literature possesses another book in which laws of the holidays, or other precepts, are presented with such fervor. The reader is also captivated by the enormous richness of thought about God, man, and Jew, which envelops the presentation of laws and customs. In addition, the author included in his book a multitude of ideas collected from ancient and medieval Jewish literature. The work thus became an anthology that offers the reader an opportunity to acquaint himself with many pious and kabbalistic books. In its totality it is one great, wondrous, and passionate call to the individual Jew to lead a life of purity and to use his spiritual strength to combat his earthly impulses. In this program of a Jewish saintly life, and in the fervor with which it is expounded, the *Shene Luhoth Haberith* surpasses the heroic program of Jewish living of the *Haside Ashkenaz,* Pious Men of Ashkenaz that we find in the famous work *Rokeah, The Ointment Maker* of Rabbi Eleazar of Worms (1165–1238).

The very title of the book and the names of its various parts are unusual too. One part is named the *Ten Commandments;* instead of having chapters, the book is divided into tractates, on the model of the Talmud. According to a folk-legend, the Jewish people tacitly resented the proud-sounding title of the book *Shene Luhoth Haberith.* The same legend also criticizes the great Maimonides for naming his code of laws *Mishneh Torah, Deuteronomy.* Another scholar, Rabbi Moses Alsheikh, a sixteenth-century biblical commentator, was the third to be taken to task for the name *Torath Mosheh, The Torah of Moses,* that he gave to his work. Popular opinion quietly decided to change the names of all these three works. Rabbi Isaiah Horovitz' work is never referred to by its full name, but is called in an abbreviated form *Shelah.*

The same people who rejected the exceedingly ambitious title accepted the contents of the book with open arms. First published in Amsterdam in 1649, the work was reprinted many times. The abridged *Shelah,* too, went through multiple editions both in Hebrew and in Yiddish. Israel Zinberg, the great historian of Jewish literature, says that though Isaiah Horovitz did not create a new, original philosophy, he was an excellent popularizer of the teachings of the great kabbalist Rabbi Isaac Luria (*Ari,* the "Lion"). Rabbi Isaiah was uniquely adept in adapting the mystical teachings of the Palestinian kabbalist to the spiritual world of the Polish Jew. He expressed the dreams of the Jew of the ghetto in tender language. The work was published at the very moment when Poland's free and prosperous Jewry was toppled by the Great Catastrophe. This further contributed to the enormous popularity of the work, which became the most beloved religious folk-book. And it is

worth noting that though the book has been called solely
by its abridged name *Shelah,* it is one of the few that the Jewish
people consider really holy. It is usually referred to as *Shelah
Hakadosh,* "The Holy Shelah."

IX.

The inclination toward oral expression manifested in the
lively pilpulistic discussions in the yeshivah and in the sermons
of the preachers was matched by an almost passionate literary
activity. The halakhist forgot his doubts as to whether he
should take a decisive position in matters of religious life as
soon as an opportunity presented itself to him to commit his
research to writing. Similarly, the *darshan* was not satisfied
with the sermons he preached to his contemporaries and felt an
urge to turn them into literary documents that would survive
him. The Men of the Renaissance found in their literary work
a welcome means of realizing their yearning for immortality.

The writings of Rabbi Ephraim Lunchits provide an interesting glimpse of the literary life of the epoch. He tells us
candidly that the urge to literary creativity caused him many
sleepless nights. His original desire was, of course, to write
works in Halakhah, the main literary field of the epoch. But
he realized that so much was being produced in this area that
there was hardly any place left for original creativity. He then
began to consider the composition of a biblical commentary.
His scholarly integrity made him aware that in this area as well
more than enough had already been written. The few attempts
in this direction he did make convinced him of the futility of
the endeavor; all "new" interpretations of biblical passages he
could think of turned out to have been already suggested. Consequently, he decided to write sermons. This was no doubt an
act of Providence, for precisely in this field Rabbi Ephraim
Lunchits was one of the few giants.

How important literary activity was to the people of that
time can be seen in the fact that the same Rabbi Ephraim

Lunchits made a solemn vow to write his *Keli Yakar* when he recovered from a dangerous illness. Others, as did Rabbi Moses Isserles in an earlier period, took to literary work when they were compelled to leave their homes during one of the frequent epidemics. Obviously, literary activity was a great consolation to these writers. Rabbi Mordecai Yaffe and Rabbi Joshua Falk were both of the opinion that literary activity was important enough to merit relinquishing even the coveted career of a rabbi or rosh yeshivah. Rabbi Mordecai Yaffe, indeed, curtailed his teaching duties in order to gain the necessary time for the composition of his great work. And Rabbi Joshua Falk vowed to reject any rabbinic position offered to him, even if it were in a very large community. He believed that an author who is serious about his work should concentrate on it and on it alone.

Besides the inner drive toward literary activity, external factors stimulated it as well. There was a pressing need for scholarly literature for the rapidly expanding yeshivah network. The above-mentioned Rabbi Nathan Shapiro, one of the better-known scholars, who served as a rabbi and rosh yeshivah in Grodno, tells us that his students urged him to compose a commentary on *Shaare Dura,* the textbook still much in use in the yeshivahs. Two generations earlier, when Rabbi Shakhna faced a similar demand from his students, he refused to do it, and consequently left a very meager literary heritage. Rabbi Nathan Shapiro did not reject such a request and composed the commentary. The change in the intellectual climate is surely also manifested in the fact that authors could more easily enlist moral support for their work and financial assistance in its publication. When the period drew to a close, no less an institution than the Council of the Four Provinces began to extend a helping hand to authors in the printing of their works.

The increased literary activity evoked the usual jealousy among authors. The dubious custom of belittling every new book upon its publication became widespread. Rabbi Ephraim Lunchits describes the dishonest methods used by the critics: "All they (i.e. the critics) think of is to search (the book) for things that could be derided. The good things, however, he (the critic) passes with silence and does not mention them." Rabbi Issachar Berman, the author of *Matenoth Kehunah,* too, reports the use of dishonest means in literary criticism.

When one looks upon this literary period from a historical viewpoint, one realizes that the writers' controversies did not cause any considerable damage, and that it was, after all, a remarkable era. The main interest was focused, as we have seen, upon halakhic literature. More than half of the books published by the printing presses of Cracow and Lublin in the last decades of the century belong to this area. The interest in sermonic literature and in kabbalistic works was vivid as well. A clear tendency towards books written in a popular vein could be noticed in every field. Most of the books by Rabbi Manoah Hendel had the avowed task of popularizing many areas of the humanities and the sciences. The importance of Isaiah Horovitz' *magnum opus* lies, to a high degree, in its popular character. Nathan Shapiro reports that when his students asked him to write the commentary on *Shaare Dura* they also requested that it be written "in a polished language and clear style, that will be easy and not hard . . . in Hebrew and not in Aramaic." Obviously, the young scholars did not like the many Aramaic words and idioms which a talmudist would usually insert into his Hebrew style. The wish was most clearly expressed by Rabbi Jehiel Michel Moravchik that the public should be offered books that they would enjoy studying. In the introduction to his *Seder Berakhoth, Order of the Blessings,* he says that it is the duty of an author to make his book attractive "by all kinds of sweetness." To achieve this purpose, he thought, an author should write in a colorful style composed of various elements, much in the manner that medicine to be given to a patient is composed of different ingredients.

X.

In the main area of literature, the Halakhah, the learned writers were very much concerned with the problem of textual

correctness in the works they were studying. We saw how in the
preceding generation Rabbi Solomon Luria had made an ear-
nest effort to cope with this problem. The result of this effort
was his important work *Hokhmath Shelomoh*. At the turn of
the century, this trend toward textual criticism, a main feature
of humanism, did not subside, but clearly reached a peak. Corrections were even suggested in the texts of liturgical poems and
in Maimonides' philosophical writings. Menahem David ben
Isaac, renowned under the name Maharam of Tykocin, systematically corrected all the books he happened to have in his
private library. This kind of activity was considered laudable;
his son was clearly enthused while reporting it. It became the
vogue to possess books that were properly corrected. Rabbi
Joseph Katz, an earlier scholar, tells us that when he intended
to publish a medieval work from a manuscript which he owned,
the Cracow printers rejected it until it was properly corrected.
Even more revealing is the statement of the Lublin printers
that, in 1574 when they prepared the tractate Avodah Zarah,
Strange Worship, Idolatry, of the Babylonian Talmud for publication, they made many efforts "to find old books." They did,
indeed, find an old manuscript of Rashi's commentary written
on parchment. By using this material they succeeded in correcting all the "damage that former printers did to the text."
Thus, almost all the leading scholars, while they devoted their
research to the interpretation of great works, were also busy
correcting the texts themselves. Rabbi Nathan Shapiro, who
wrote his commentary on *Shaare Dura* at the request of his
students, simultaneously corrected its text, because the copies
at his disposal "turned out to be full of errors." Rabbi Joshua
Falk used Moses Isserles' original manuscript to correct the
printed editions of the *Mappah*. And Rabbi Meir of Lublin,
who was a great admirer of the Tosafoth, was preoccupied with
the correction of their texts.

The corrections to the Talmud proposed by Rabbi Solomon
Luria, and subsequently introduced by the printers into the
text, turned out to be unsatisfactory to the scholars of the next
generation. This is why the above mentioned scholar-popular-

izer Manoah Hendel suggested additional corrections in the Talmud. Just as Luria's Talmudic corrections were collected after his death by his heirs and published under the title *Hokhmath Shelomoh,* Manoah Hendel's son, too, named the results of his father's research *Hokhmath Manoah, Wisdom of Manoah.* In the introduction to this work the author's son states cautiously, but not without exaggeration, that though Solomon Luria succeeded in correcting all the errors, new damage was done to the text by the printers, especially by the publishers of the Cracow edition of the Talmud. His father's objective was to correct these new inaccuracies in the Talmudic text. *Hokhmath Manoah* like *Hokhmath Shelomoh* is a work collected posthumously from notes that Rabbi Manoah Hendel made in the margin of his own copy of the Talmud.

Open criticism of Rabbi Solomon Luria's corrections in the Talmud came from Rabbi Meir of Lublin. Rabbi Samuel Edels went even further and sharply attacked the whole trend of correcting the Talmud, as grossly exaggerated and unnecessary. He argued that "the old text is correct" and that it is the "corrections" that damage it. To be sure, he did not mention Solomon Luria by name. But, when he attacked the publishers of the "recent editions" of the Talmud, who permitted themselves to introduce corrections into the text proper, everyone knew against whom his criticism was directed. He demanded that proposed corrections should be printed in the margin, but that the text of the Talmud proper should not be changed. When Rabbi Samuel himself found it necessary to suggest some textual corrections, he did so only with regard to the commentaries on the Talmud, and especially the Tosafoth. But he never asked to have the text actually adjusted in accordance with his suggestions; rather, they were part of his great commentary on the Talmud, of which more will be said later. The irony was that the printers of Lublin, who like their Cracow colleagues, tampered with the text of the Talmud, did so by inserting the corrections suggested by him into the text. The basically sound tendency of the scholars to suggest textual improvements based upon old, good manuscripts, and on their own deeper understanding of the Talmud and its main commentaries, certainly got out of hand. At this point Rabbi Samuel Edels asserted his great authority to confine again the "correction efforts" to reasonable limits.

XI.

The two greatest authors of the epoch were Rabbi Meir of Lublin and Rabbi Samuel Edels. The older of the two, Rabbi Meir ben Gedalyah entered history under the name of Maharam of Lublin. He was born in 1558 into a rabbinic family. The rosh yeshivah of Cracow, Rabbi Asher, author of a kabbalistic book, was his ancestor. While a folk-legend has it that at the age of eight Meir knew several tractates of the Talmud by heart, the records tell us only that young Meir studied in Cracow in a yeshivah headed by Rabbi Isaac Shapiro. Like Moses Isserles he, too, married the daughter of his master. All his life Meir of Lublin felt grateful to and proud of his teacher and father-in-law. His signature usually carries the phrase "son-in-law of the king Rabbi Isaac," in accordance with the custom of calling a great scholar "king" (comp. Gittin 62a).

As a very young man Meir achieved great fame. In the course of time he became the rabbi or the rosh yeshivah in the three most important communities in the Commonwealth: his hometown of Lublin, Cracow, and Lemberg. His first position was probably that of a rosh yeshivah in Cracow, which he accepted in the late 1580's. He held it for a decade, and left for Lemberg before the year 1600. There, too, Meir held the position of a rosh yeshivah for about fifteen years. At that time another yeshivah existed in Lemberg, under the guidance of Rabbi Joshua Falk. After a number of years a conflict developed between the two learned men. The conflict grew in intensity— as was usual among the humanists—and Meir was compelled to leave the city. He then returned to Lublin, to assume the position of communal rabbi. He held this position only a few years and died in 1616 at the age of 58.

Maharam was not a scholar who withdrew from active life for the purpose of study. On the contrary, he was very involved in communal affairs, and he clearly derived great satisfaction from this activity. His yeshivahs had the largest student bodies known at the time in similar institutions. His responsa frequently express his deep personal interest in his educational institutions. In addition, he was very active in the Council of the Four Provinces, and steadily participated in its sessions and decisions. Meir's communal interests were also manifested in his desire that more and more people might turn to him with questions pertaining to the Jewish law. This explicit quest for the opportunity to issue legal opinions is unique in the vast responsa literature of the Jewish people.

In general Rabbi Meir of Lublin was a typical man of the Renaissance, proud—probably too proud—of his knowledge, and insistent that proper recognition be given to him. He felt absolutely sure that his decisions in matters of Halakhah represented the ultimate truth and he reacted sharply to any dissenting opinion. The uncompromising and often offensive language which he used against his opponents was uncommon in Poland. His invective resembles the language of the perpetually feuding Italian-Jewish humanists. For example, when a German rabbi refused to accept a decision rendered by him, Rabbi Meir conceived a plan in the manner of the Italian humanists to depose this opponent from his rabbinic position. Obviously, only his true greatness in learning persuaded his contemporaries to overlook these shortcomings. Many of the great rabbis, and among them the venerable Mordecai Yaffe, came to his support during one of his sharpest feuds. Another rabbi, of the prominent community of Ostrog, in his enthusiasm said that "if all the scholars of Poland and Reussen (i.e. southeastern Poland) were put on one scale, and the gaon Rabbi Meir on the other one, he would outweigh all of them together."

Although Meir of Lublin was perpetually busy with his yeshivah and with communal affairs, he was a prolific writer. According to his son, Rabbi Meir wrote five works, besides his many responsa. In his later years he planned an exposition of the whole world of Jewish religious law, thought, and deed. Unfortunately, he died before the work was completed.

What puzzles us is that such a self-centered personality as Meir of Lublin made no attempt to publish his works during his lifetime. Of all his works, only the commentary on the Talmud was published after his death under the name *Meir Ene Hakhamim, (The Book that) Enlightens the Eyes of the Scholars.* A selection of 140 responsa was also published under an almost identical title *Manhir Ene Hakhamim.* Meir's other works, still unpublished, include a collection of sermons and commentaries on almost all the textbooks studied in the yeshivahs.

Rabbi Meir of Lublin gained for himself a niche in the history of Jewish literature with his *Meir Ene Hakhamim,* a systematic commentary on the Talmud. This commentary and a similar work by Rabbi Samuel Edels together curbed for a short time the rising tide of the literary efforts of the halakhists on the *Shulhan Arukh.* Meir was an avowed opponent of this type of Rabbinic literature, and he refused to consult it when he prepared his halakhic opinions. "It is not my custom, or my method," he writes, "to study the opinions of the authors of the *Shulhan Arukh,* and still less to base a halakhic judgment on . . . their words, because they are not derived from one source. . . . " His opposition to the *Shulhan Arukh* even extended to the *Raiments,* the lifework of Rabbi Mordecai Yaffe whom he greatly revered as the dean of the Polish scholars. Meir's ambition was to learn the Jewish law directly from the Talmud and its early commentators. His desire also was to reach the true interpretation of the law through independent research.

An analysis of Maharam's method of study reveals a constant effort to understand the simple, direct meaning of a text. He found that a good means to attain this goal was to read the short, lively glossae of the Tosafists. His admiration for the Tosafists was so great that he devoted the main part of the work to them. His commentary on the Talmud thus became a super-commentary on the Tosafists and also partly on Rashi, rather than directly upon the Talmud. His style is simple. In order to fully clarify his thought, he likes to elaborate upon a problem from many angles. The style he employed in the *Responsa* is much different. Here his statements are concise and always devoid of theoretical digression.

The *Meir Ene Hakhamim* was published the first time in 1618 in Venice, and immediately gained the status of an accepted commentary on the Talmud. It was later republished many times. But its universal character is manifested in the fact that it has been printed in virtually all the Talmud editions as one of its few principal commentaries.

XII.

The other great commentator on the Talmud in this epoch was Rabbi Samuel Elizer ben Judah Halevi, known as the Maharsha. He was a contemporary of Meir of Lublin, but may have been a few years his senior. He lived well into the seventeenth century (1631). It seems, that Samuel spent most of his life in Posen where he married into a wealthy and scholarly family. He himself belonged to a scholarly family that descended, according to a tradition, from Rabbi Judah the Pious, the famous moralist who lived in Germany in the early thirteenth century.

We do not possess much information about the Maharsha's formative years. In 1590 he was asked to add his signature to an important document issued by the Council of the Four Provinces. This fact indicates that he was a recognized scholar by then. Earlier, in the 1580's his mother-in-law, Edel Ashkenazi, put at his disposal the means for opening a yeshivah. She maintained the school for about twenty years. The Maharsha extended proper recognition to his mother-in-law for her good deeds by including her name in his signature: Samuel Edels. The good woman thus earned admission to history alongside her son-in-law. After Edel's death the yeshivah closed, and Rabbi Samuel accepted the post of Rabbi of Chelm. In 1615 Rabbi Samuel was called to Lublin, where he occupied the twin positions of rabbi and rosh yeshivah for a decade. The last few years of his life he held the same two positions in Ostrog, a leading community in Volhynia. It is hard to say why Rabbi Samuel left his important post in Lublin to occupy a similar position in a less important community. It is possible that it was easier to maintain a large yeshivah in Ostrog. This yeshivah, indeed, gained great fame, and its student body was one of the largest ever recorded in Poland.

Rabbi Samuel was a moderate regarding pedagogic methodology. He was of the opinion that a student should be trained in the method of the Pilpul in order to gain the skill of analyzing a problem. On the other hand, he sharply opposed the type of Pilpul called *Hilluk,* because it was a "pilpul of vanity." He refused to accept the acrobatics of the mind that could "interpret" a text in which a part was missing.

In the first years of the seventeenth century Rabbi Samuel Edels' fame continued to grow, both because of his scholarship and his moral stature. His generosity was expressed in a verse from Job (31:32) engraved at the entrance to his home: "The stranger did not lodge in the street; My doors I opened to the roadside." The house with the inscription still stood at the end of the nineteenth century. Many legends were alive then, and are still alive today, in which people express their admiration for his learning and piety.

The greatest literary heritage that Rabbi Samuel Edels left to posterity is his twin commentaries on the Talmud, *Hiddushe Halakhoth Wehiddushe Aggadoth, Commentary on the Halakhah and Aggadah (in the Talmud).* This work was the result of decades of instruction in the yeshivah. Few rabbinic scholars used the classroom as a research laboratory in the Talmud to the extent that Rabbi Samuel did. He perpetually discussed Talmudic problems with his students and colleagues. He refrained from writing his commentary on a certain part of the tractate Sabbath, because when this material was studied, he was absent from the yeshivah. His scholarly integrity is fully manifested by the character of his commentary to the tractate Nedarim, Vows. He realized that the older commentaries on this tractate, including the Tosafoth, are full of textual errors. He then devoted his commentary to correcting these errors, but refrained from writing a new commentary on it.

Rabbi Samuel's stern method of research and the depth of his mind make his one of the most original commentaries on the Talmud. Most of his comments are in effect an effort to elucidate the simple meaning of a passage through the use of the vast sources contained within the Talmud itself. He himself said that his perpetual search was for the *or hapeshat,* the light contained in the simple explanation. Quite often his analytical mind questioned what were considered historical facts. In his effort to focus his words on the *peshat,* he always tried to formulate his thoughts as concisely as possible. In this he, no doubt, went too far and made it into a difficult commentary. His work was therefore studied solely by an elite group of Talmudic scholars. Some parts in it are so obscure that even great scholars are unable to penetrate them completely.

This manner of commenting on the halakhic parts of the Talmud was original at least to a certain degree. Rabbi Samuel Edels was truly original when he extended his commentary to the Talmudic Aggadah. An overwhelming majority of the Talmudic scholars of all times devoted their work, both as teachers and as authors, exclusively to the Halakhah. Normative Jewry was always so much in need of halakhic guidance that its intellectual forces were mobilized to spread the knowledge of the Halakhah and to apply its principles to the ever-changing conditions. Giving in to the needs of everyday life, the scholars often tended to forget that the Talmud is also a great storehouse of ideals that should be employed to raise the moral stature of the people. The preachers, of course, made wide use of this material for their purposes. But rabbis and heads of yeshivahs generally confined themselves to the exclusive study of the Halakhah. Rabbi Samuel Edels was a rosh yeshivah, in fact one of the greatest among them. His reputation as a halakhist has survived, undimmed by the centuries. Yet he did not feel satisfied by his achievements in halakhic research. He was keenly aware of the faults of his generation, and sought to remedy the situation by the use of the aggadic material of the Talmud as a means of education. "From the Aggadah," he says, "one can learn ways of ethical behavior, wisdom, and how to instruct the people." He therefore wrote the commentary to the Talmudic Aggadah, and clearly considered it as important as his celebrated commentary on the Talmudic Halakhah. He originally composed this work as a commentary on the aggadic material collected in the famous anthology *En Yaakov, Well of Jacob* by Rabbi Jacob ibn Habib, an exile from Spain. In addition, he interpreted all the aggadic material that Rabbi Jacob ibn Habib failed to include into his anthology. Rabbi Samuel's commentary on the Aggadah thus became a basic guide in this field. To interpret the Aggadah, Maharsha employed various means. He interpreted some of the tales and legends in a rational manner; to others he applied an allegorical method. He also made an effort to clarify the fantastic, obscure tales to which modern scholarship finds the key in the Greco-Roman culture that dominated the Near East in the era of the Rabbis. Maharsha was not versed in Hellenistic culture and history. But in his own way he tried to give acceptable interpretations to all those bizarre stories and statements.

Maharsha considered both parts of his commentary equally important and planned to integrate them into one work. This is the reason why many editions of the Talmud printed both commentaries together as a running text. The publishers, however, were not fully converted to the idea of the equality of both parts of the work; consequently the commentary on the Aggadah is usually printed in a smaller type than the one used for the Halakhah. The first edition of a part of the *Hiddushe Halakhoth* began to be set in print the first day of Hanukah, 1611, and about ten years later an additional part of the work was published. The author kept on improving his work all through the later years of his life and produced a revised version of it. Only a part of this new version was later published by Rabbi Samuel Edels' son-in-law. Most of the revised version, however, was destroyed in the storm of the Great Catastrophe.

The work of Rabbi Samuel Edels quickly gained unusual recognition, and has always been considered superior to the similar works of Rabbi Solomon Luria and Rabbi Meir of Lublin. A modern historian of Rabbinic literature questions the superiority of Rabbi Samuel's work and is amazed by its great success. A fact is, however, that both the *vox populi* and the *vox scholarum* declared the *Hiddushe Halakhot Wehiddushe Aggadoth* the greatest work produced in East European Rabbinic literature. At the beginning of the eighteenth century, a scholar of Prague advised his sons to diligently study Maharsha's work, because "God's spirit speaks in it," and without having attained "divine inspiration no man could produce a work of this kind." When the scholar-traveler Hayim Joseph David Azulai visited Amsterdam in 1778, an immigrant from Poland related several popular legends to him that had grown up about the work. Till this very day one who studies the Talmud with the commentary of Maharsha is considered a true scholar. Yehezkel Kotik tells in *Meine Zikhroynes, My Reminiscences,* that in his young years, more than a century ago, capable men who studied this work were commonly referred to as Maharsha *keplech,* i.e., Maharsha minds. This, more than anything else, testifies to the universality of the belief that Rabbi Samuel Edels' commentary on the Talmud constitutes the supreme achievement of the Jewish mind in Eastern Europe.

XIII.

We have seen how the two greatest scholars of the epoch, Rabbi Meir of Lublin and Rabbi Samuel Edels, both opposed the "codes literature" as a matter of principle. We also acknowledged the setback this opposition caused to the study of the codes in the yeshivahs. Nevertheless, the epoch produced much literature of this kind. Maharam's desire that every rabbi obtain the answers to problems of the religious law directly from the Talmud was no more than a dream. It was beyond the capabilities of the average rabbi, even if he obtained his training during years of studying in a yeshivah. The realities of Jewish life required the rabbis to have a rich variety of codes at their disposal. That the need for codes was satisfactorily answered is evident in the fact that when Rabbi Ephraim Lunchits planned to compose a book of this type, he was amazed to find that there were "too many" of them. Many of the leading rabbis, and also some of the less prominent ones, contributed to this area of literature. Rabbi Nathan Shapiro of Grodno and Manoah Hendel, the prolific writer, both wrote commentaries on the *Arbaah Turim.* These commentaries were never published, for reasons unknown to us. The very fact, however, that they were written, and that their authors were a famous rosh yeshivah and a great writer-popularizer, shows that they fulfilled a real need. Rabbi Nathan Shapiro also felt the need to facilitate the formulation of halakhic decisions when he wrote the above-mentioned commentary on *Shaare Dura.* He added information about the varied practice of each law upon which he commented, in different countries such as Poland, Ukraine, Lithuania, Germany, Bohemia, and Moravia. Maharam of Tykocin, also a well-known scholar, wrote short comments on the *Alfasi,* an older Sephardic code of laws. Descriptions of laws composed in rhymed prose also appeared then. In his book Rabbi Isaac Hayes presented the laws of Passover in rhymed prose. Similarly, Rabbi Moses the Dead, the author of the remarkable work *Matte Mosheh,* described the six hundred and thirteen Jewish precepts in rhymes. Decisions in complicated cases were, of course, arrived at by soliciting the opinions of leading jurists. This epoch, indeed, left a larger heritage of Rabbinic responsa than the preceding decades, though not as rich as could be expected. Outstanding among them are the Responsa of Rabbi Meir of Lublin and the collection *Masath Binyamin, Benjamin's Portion* (comp. Genesis 43:34) by Rabbi Benjamin Solnik. Rabbi Benjamin's Responsa are a model of well organized and clear legal opinions.

An important and acute problem that called for urgent rabbinic action was the credit operations of the Jews in Poland. The laws that prohibit a Jew from lending money to another

Jew on interest are a part of the section Yoreh Deah, The
Teaching of Knowledge (comp. Isaiah 28:9)of the *Shulhan
Arukh*. The prohibition of interest was considered a matter of
ritual rather than a problem of civil law. With Jewish economic
life in Eastern Europe in those times becoming more and more
dynamic, credit transactions between Jew and Jew became inevitable. There was a real danger that many people would
transgress the prohibition on interest. The religious leadership
began to search therefore for an economic formula that would
make it possible for Jews to conduct their business activity
without directly violating the anti-usury laws. As a result, this
problem became a central theme in the responsa literature and
it also was placed on the agenda of the Council of the Four
Provinces. The combined efforts of rabbinic and lay leadership
resulted in a code of practice that was adopted at a meeting
of rashe yeshivoth in Lublin in 1607. Rabbi Joshua Falk of
Lemberg was charged with the formulation of the code, and
the *Kuntres Hasema,* so called after Joshua Falk's literary
name, was incorporated in the official minute book of the
Council. Somewhat earlier, however, the formula known as
Heter Iska, Instrument to Trade on Shares, proposed by the
rabbi of Cracow, Rabbi Mendel ben Avigdor, became universally accepted. It has served ever since as the basis for credit
transactions among Jews who do not wish to transgress the
grave prohibition of usury in Jewish law.

Aside from these contemporary law books, the *Shulhan
Arukh* remained popular, despite opposition of the two giants
of the Halakhah, Rabbi Meir of Lublin and Rabbi Samuel
Edels. When Rabbi Nathan Shapiro wanted to claim that in
his work *Mevo Shearim, Entrance to the Gates,* he prepared the
laws very clearly, he said that the book is "like a *Table Prepared* (*Shulhan Arukh*) for (my) students."

The above-mentioned Rabbi Benjamin Solnik considered
the *Beth Yosef* of Rabbi Joseph Karo, the mother work of
the *Shulhan Arukh,* the book upon which the totality of Jewish
societal life is founded. The popular Yiddish writer Jacob of
Yanov, author of the beloved folk book *Tseenah Ureenah,* also

composed an index to the contents and sources of the Yoreh
Deah section of the *Shulhan Arukh*. Even Joshua Falk who,
as we shall see later, had many objections to the *Shulhan
Arukh*, nevertheless recognized the fact that Rabbi Moses Isserles' addenda to it (*Mappah*) transformed it into a religious
guide for Polish Jewry. He repeatedly stressed the fact that the
Shulhan Arukh, in the form in which it was studied at the end
of the sixteenth century, is a common work of Rabbi Joseph
Karo and Rabbi Moses Isserles. We find similar thoughts in
the writings of Rabbi Mordecai Yaffe. Mordecai Yaffe and
Joshua Falk were the authors of the two great codes produced
at that time. In the literature of the codes, they earned a position of significance similar to that occupied by Rabbi Meir of
Lublin and Rabbi Samuel Edels in the field of Talmudic commentaries.

XIV.

Rabbi Mordecai Yaffe was born in Prague in Bohemia in
1530 into a wealthy and distinguished family. He came to
Poland as a lad and studied under Solomon Luria and Moses
Isserles. He took instruction in Jewish mystic lore from one of
the great kabbalists. In addition, he found some time for the
study of philosophy and of the mathematical sciences. After
having spent a couple of years in Poland, the young scholar
returned to Prague and opened a yeshivah. The political situation of the Jews in Prague at that time was not too favorable,
and they lived under perpetual threat of expulsion. Many
Jews became impatient with the situation and began to emigrate. We find the young scholar Mordecai Yaffe among the
emigrants of 1561. He went to Italy and plunged again into
study, this time of secular disciplines. He returned to Poland
in the early 1570's where he remained most of his long life.
He occupied the positions of rabbi and rosh yeshivah in several
large communities in the east and finally in Posen, where he
spent his last years. He died at the age of 82 in 1612.

During all the years Rabbi Mordecai Yaffe lived in Poland, and especially about the year 1600, he was held in high esteem. He was much older than the other distinguished rashe yeshivoth and rabbis and was considered their dean. He belonged to the highest leadership of the Council of the Four Provinces and also gained the fame of a great preacher. A contemporary author of a chronicle describes him as "head and leader of scholars and judges of the Three (Four) Provinces."

The years that Mordecai Yaffe spent in Rabbi Moses Isserles' school, and the decade he studied in Italy, made him a typical man of the Renaissance. While he was an ardent student of the secular sciences, and admired the rationalist philosopher Moses Maimonides like most of the men of the Renaissance, he also believed in various superstitions. The culture of the Renaissance also implanted within him its admirable values, above all a yearning for harmony. The search for harmony strongly influenced his outlook and his method of study. His scientific mind tended to reject the extreme forms of the Pilpul. He nevertheless sought to reconcile and harmonize the contradictory opinions of various Talmudic jurists. He admired Rashi's commentaries and consistently defended them against their critics. Much like his teacher Moses Isserles, he thought highly of the *minhag,* the folk-usage, as an important element of the Halakhah. The impression is clear that of his two teachers, the harmonious and conciliatory Rabbi Moses Isserles had a considerably greater influence upon the formation of his personality than the dialectical, ever-critical Rabbi Solomon Luria.

All these tendencies reveal themselves in Mordecai Yaffe's ten-volume work *Levush Malkhuth, The Royal Raiment.* The title of the work contains a reference to the author's name (comp. Esther 8:15, and *Mordecai* went forth from the presence of the king in *royal apparel* etc.). The titles of the individual volumes were taken from the same biblical passage.

Rabbi Mordecai Yaffe had a passion for writing. He went so far as to curtail his classes in order to write. The typical author in him is shown by the deep sorrow that the lack of money to publish his collection of sermons *Levush Simhah Wesason, The Raiment of Gladness and Joy* (comp. Esther 8:16) caused him. It seems that over the decades his family's wealth diminished. In his literary career Rabbi Mordecai Yaffe encountered unusual difficulties. At a relatively young age he embarked upon the composition of a legal handbook to be used by religious leaders in their daily practice. The publication of the *Beth Yosef* completely upset his plan. He thought, as did Ephraim Lunchits somewhat later, that there was no place now for additional legal compendia. Yet, a careful analysis of Rabbi Joseph Karo's work convinced him that his doubts were unfounded, and that he should proceed with his original plans. To begin with, he realized that Karo always follows the decisions of Maimonides as was customary in the Near Eastern countries. European Jewry, however, had its own Halakhah and customs. In addition, he thought that *Beth Yosef* was too voluminous to serve as a handy reference book. Consequently, he set out to write a more concise manual that would also embody the Ashkenazic Halakhah. Then, however, the news reached him that Rabbi Joseph Karo had been working himself on a digest of the *Beth Yosef,* the *Shulhan Arukh.* Rabbi Mordecai Yaffe again had no choice but to stop the work that he had begun.

When the *Shulhan Arukh* was finally published, Rabbi Mordecai Yaffe realized that his decision to interrupt his work had been too hasty. He saw that Joseph Karo went much too far in his work of abridgement. In addition, the *Shulhan Arukh* also failed to take into consideration Western Jewry's religious usages. Hence, he returned to his interrupted work again. But than a new blow threatened to shatter his literary plans. He found out that his own teacher, Rabbi Moses Isserles, was working on the composition of the *Mappah,* designed to be an Ashkenazic supplement to the *Shulhan Arukh.* The much interrupted work had, of course, to be interrupted again, at least until the character of the *Mappah* should become known. But when the *Mappah* was published Mordecai Yaffe realized that this work, too, did not remedy the major shortcoming of the *Shulhan Arukh*—its being too much of an abridgement. He strongly believed that the students of the yeshivahs were in need of a more comprehensive description of the Jewish law. Now he clearly saw his task: "and this my book," he writes, "shall be a work in the middle between the two extremes." The "extremes" are the too voluminous *Beth Yosef* and the excessively brief *Shulhan Arukh*.

Rabbi Mordecai Yaffe returned with new vigor to his work and this time completed it. It occupies five of the ten *Raiments* that constitute his entire literary work. He modeled his halakhic work entirely after the *Shulhan Arukh*. It has the same division and each part is divided into the same number of paragraphs. Nevertheless, the differences between the books are impressive. The *Shulhan Arukh* lists the various laws in a brief and concise manner, without indicating their sources in the Torah or in the Talmud and without presenting their underlying ideas. The *Raiments,* instead, offers a well-rounded description of the various laws, presented with literary skill and in a crisp and readable style. A comparison of any paragraph in the *Raiments* with its counterpart in the *Shulhan Arukh* proves that Rabbi Mordecai Yaffe plowed deeply into the material that he found in the *Beth Yosef* and in other sources, and that his work is not a mere technical compilation, but a new, original work.

Rabbi Mordecai Yaffe thus achieved his coveted goal. His great wish was that his work should become a basic textbook for the yeshivahs. And the book, indeed, attained wide use. Even in the Holy Land where the *Shulhan Arukh* was written, the *Raiments* enjoyed unusual popularity. While Mordecai Yaffe was still alive, it became customary, in Jerusalem, to study the *Raiments* after the morning prayers.

The other five parts of the *Royal Raiments* contain Rabbi Mordecai Yaffe's writings in Pentateuchal exegesis, philosophy, and homiletics. A description of these works will be provided below. Here it should be added that the popularity of the *Raiments* as a code was considerable but of short duration. Various reasons contributed to this. To begin with, Rabbi Meir of Lublin, though a great admirer of Rabbi Mordecai

Yaffe, opposed the work simply because it was a code. In addition, the older generation of scholars looked down upon it because they thought that it was written in too popular a vein. The clarity of the presentation, the orderly arrangement of the material, and the space given to the sources of the laws and their formulation certainly appealed to the non-professional, non-sophisticated student of the Jewish law. About two hundred years later, Rabbi Mordecai Yaffe found a great imitator of his method. When Shneur Zalman of Lyady, the great leader of the Hasidim in White Russia, decided to write a new *Shulhan Arukh,* he arranged his work on the model of the *Raiments.* In 1600, however, the rabbis did not consider it "scholarly" enough. Even Rabbi Joshua Falk, who authored a code of laws himself, opposed the *Raiments* sharply and indoctrinated his students against it. The opposition of Rabbi Joshua Falk and his school played no small part in bringing about the eclipse of the popularity of the *Raiments* in the yeshivahs.

XV.

Rabbi Joshua Falk ben Alexander Hacohen was much younger than Rabbi Mordecai Yaffe. But he, too, could still get instruction from the two great teachers of the preceding generation. He first studied under Rabbi Moses Isserles, who was his relative, and later became a pupil of Rabbi Solomon Luria. Of utmost importance in his life was the fact that he became a son-in-law of the wealthy leader of Lemberg's Jewish community, Israel Jozefowicz. His wife Bella was herself highly educated and was responsible for a number of comments on matters of Jewish law later discussed among the scholars. The father-in-law was a magnanimous philanthropist. He built synagogues in various towns and aided many of the needy in Poland and in the Holy Land.

The wealth and understanding of the father-in-law made it possible for Joshua to start a scholarly career in the way he wished. As we have seen above, Joshua Falk was convinced that the generally followed custom of combining the positions of the communal rabbi and rosh yeshivah was not beneficial to research. He was of the opinion that a scholar who wanted to head a yeshivah and to pursue literary work in the *halakhah* should be free of the manifold daily duties of a communal functionary. Consequently, Israel Jozefowicz offered to finance a yeshivah for his son-in-law so that he would not be dependent upon the salary of a communal rabbi for a livelihood. He started building a magnificent three-story stone house as a facility for the school. He then provided for the needs of his son-in-law and the students of the school for a full quarter of a century. The building stood for about two hundred and fifty years. It was demolished by a fire in 1837. Rabbi Joshua Falk deeply appreciated all that his father-in-law had done for him. He expressed his gratitude by naming a trilogy of his works for him, *Beth Israel, The House of Israel.*

Rabbi Joshua Falk attained high esteem in rabbinic circles. He frequently attended sessions of the Council of the Four Provinces. We have seen that the Council entrusted him with the formulation of the decisions on the laws on interest it issued in 1607. A stormy moment in his life came in 1610 when he arranged a divorce during a visit to Vienna. Rabbi Meir of Lublin, who at the time headed another yeshivah in Lemberg, declared the divorce illegal. A heated debate on this issue virtually divided the Rabbinate into two warring camps. Rabbi Meir was ultimately compelled to leave Lemberg. Joshua Falk died in Lemberg in 1614.

Joshua Falk considered his literary work as important as the yeshivah, perhaps more so. He recorded all the observations on legal problems that resulted from discussions with his pupils in his notebooks. In other words, he systematically collected material for his works. His scholarly interests were manifold. Like his friend Manoah Hendel, he, too, wrote in the areas of Halakhah, mysticism, philosophy, and the sciences. His writings, however, had a sad fate. A large part of them, possibly most of them, were destroyed in two fires, one during the author's lifetime, the other two years after his death. Joshua's

rich library was also a victim of the fires. Consequently, all of
the valuable notes and comments written in the margins of his
books were also destroyed. Of his many responsa, about one
hundred and forty survived. But even these were never published as a book.

The literary heritage of Rabbi Joshua Falk that has survived
is contained in four books: three books under the common
title *Beth Israel,* that are both a commentary on the *Arbaah
Turim* and a continuation of it; and the *Sefer Meirath Enaim,
The Book that Enlightens the Eyes* (comp. Psalms 19:9), an
uncompleted commentary on the *Shulhan Arukh.* The three
works of the *Beth Israel* group are named *Perishah, Commentary; Derishah, Research;* and *Hosafah, Addenda.* The *Perishah*
and *Derishah* are a twin commentary on the *Arbaah Turim.* It
was Joshua Falk's opinion that there was no adequate commentary on this widely used textbook; he, therefore, set out to
fill this gap. In the *Perishah* he systematically explained the
Tur, both on the basis of the material presented in Joseph
Karo's *Beth Yosef* and his own research. In the *Derishah* he
discussed the sources of the various laws of the *Tur* in the Talmud and in the older code literature. In the latter part he also
presented the reasons that led him often to a decision deviating
from the opinions of Rabbi Joseph Karo and Rabbi Moses
Isserles. The *Perishah* is, of course, longer than the *Derishah.*
The major research effort, however, was invested in the composition of the *Derishah.* It is a sort of a scholarly apparatus
to the work as a whole. The third book of the *Beth Israel* group
is known under various names: *Hosafah,* as mentioned above;
Beurim, Explanations; or *Tosafoth,* also meaning *Addenda.* In
this book the author described the variations of Jewish laws
formulated in Jewish jurisprudence after the composition of
the *Tur,* and especially in his own generation. Joshua Falk
gave decades of his life to the composition of the *Beth Israel*
trilogy. He revised and rewrote it several times. But he
achieved his goal, for the trilogy is now considered by the
scholarly world as the perfect commentary to the *Arbaah Turim.*

Rabbi Joshua Falk believed that just as he provided the *Tur* with a systematic scholarly commentary, it was also his duty to write a similar work on the *Shulhan Arukh* that had become the most widely used reference work of the rabbinical practitioner. As mentioned above, he was critical of Rabbi Mordecai Yaffe's *Raiments*. He accused the older scholar of not having penetrated deeply enough into the sources of the Halakhah. He therefore commenced writing a systematic commentary to the *Shulhan Arukh* which he somewhat proudly named *Sefer Meirath Enaim*. The work, popular under the abbreviated name *Sema*, offers a systematic explanation of the *Shulhan Arukh*, paragraph by paragraph. In addition, Joshua Falk was able to correct many errors that crept into Rabbi Moses Isserles' work on the *Shulhan Arukh, Mappah,* on the basis of the original *Mappah* manuscript in his possession. The *Sema* was completed only on one of the four parts of the *Shulhan Arukh,* namely the Hoshen Mishpat, Breastplate of Judgment (comp. Exodus 28:15), that describes the Jewish civil law. The commentary to the three other parts remained unwritten.

Rabbi Joshua Falk was so thoroughly convinced that the *Sema* was the definitive commentary on the *Shulhan Arukh* that he even ventured to suggest that it should not be permissible to make decisions in matters of Jewish religion and law based on the *Shulhan Arukh* without consulting the *Sema*. It was his explicit wish that the *Sema* should not be printed independently, but rather beside the *Shulhan Arukh*. It is true, indeed, that the *Sema,* written in a facile Hebrew, is the best of the many commentaries on the *Shulhan Arukh*. It is, in addition, one of the few that do not need a super-commentary to be fully comprehensible. And yet, the *Sema* did not gain the acceptance it deserved. It is hard to say why. Some are of the opinion that this is due to the fragmentary nature of the book.

Thus the problem of the *Shulhan Arukh* remained unsolved all through this period. Rabbi Meir of Lublin and Rabbi Samuel Edels, opponents of the *Shulhan Arukh,* were not able to neutralize its influence; and the works of its commentators Rabbi Mordecai Yaffe and Rabbi Joshua Falk did not bring about its acceptance. It was only in the seventeenth century that a series of commentaries was composed by several scholars that terminated the long and painful process by which the *Shulhan Arukh* was ultimately accepted by East European Jewry.

XVI.

The daily life of the Jew was the source of the intensive pre-occupation with halakhic literature. The Jew's program for the Sabbath day, instead, called for the study of the Pentateuch. The reading of the weekly portion of the Pentateuch was the central part of the Sabbath service. The average Jew, who was daily engaged in pursuit of his livelihood, used the Sabbath day to study the Pentateuch. He also made an effort to attain a deeper understanding of Holy Writ by studying it with the help of various commentaries.

During this period Polish Jewry's greatest contribution to the exegesis of the Pentateuch was made by the preachers. After an author turned a series of sermons into a literary document, it most often resulted in a more or less systematic commentary on the Pentateuch. There were also, of course, those Pentateuch commentaries that did not originate in the form of sermons. It is generally somewhat difficult to determine whether all written "sermons" were ever actually preached in a synagogue, or were rather collections of brilliant commentaries on various parts of the Pentateuch.

At any rate, the demand for the commentaries on the Penta-teuch was strong. The printing presses of Cracow and Lublin published scores of them during this period. To be sure, Rabbi Ephraim Lunchits, the great preacher, complained that the contemporary literature in this area was not sufficiently original and too often quoted older authors. A trend was nevertheless noticeable among the authors not to accept the Pentateuchal exegesis of former generations without criticism. Commentators were encouraged to contribute something new in this area as

well. That creativity was possible is amply evident in the
writings of Rabbi Ephraim Lunchits himself.

A considerable part of the exegesis produced during this
epoch does not treat the Pentateuch proper, but rather Rashi's
commentary upon it. The custom of studying the Pentateuch
with the aid of this classical commentary established itself so
firmly that the new exegesis had to use it as a point of depar-
ture. Some of the most illustrious authors of the epoch, such
as Rabbi Mordecai Yaffe and Rabbi Nathan Shapiro, wrote
just such super-commentaries on Rashi. Nathan Shapiro, in
his book *Imre Shefer, Goodly Words* (comp. Genesis 49:21),
went so far as to give more than ample attention to another
super-commentary on Rashi, that of Rabbi Elijah Mizrahi, a
great rabbi of Constantinople of the fifteenth and sixteenth
centuries. Rabbi Mordecai Yaffe made it his practice for a full
forty-five years to make notes of his observations on Rashi's
commentary when he studied the weekly portion of the Pentateuch. In his old age he collected and arranged all of this
material in one of the ten parts of his great work, *Raiments*.

The most important work of Pentateuchal exegesis was written by an immigrant from the Near East, Rabbi Eliezer Ashkenazi. He was born in 1513 somewhere in the Near East,
the son of a doctor. His name, Ashkenazi, indicates that the
family was of West European origin. Leading oriental scholars,
among them Rabbi Joseph Karo himself, were his teachers.
As a young man Eliezer was appointed a judge at the Rabbinic
court in Cairo, Egypt. He held this position for more than
twenty years. Some event, unknown to us, compelled him to
leave Egypt together with his family. Legends circulated in
Poland that the rabbi's speedy exodus from Egypt occurred in
the Pesach night during the Seder, and that a strong wind
miraculously transported him and his family instantly to Cracow, where he could complete the interrupted Seder. The historical records, however, tell us that from Egypt Eliezer Ashkenazi went to the island of Cyprus, then under the control of
the Republic of Venice. A young man from Italy became acquainted with him in 1563 on his way to the Holy Land. He

was so impressed with Rabbi Eliezer's personality that he interrupted his trip in order to study with him for several years.

When the island of Cyprus was captured by the Turks in 1571, Rabbi Eliezer Ashkenazi settled in Venice. Here a conflict arose between him and the chief rabbi of the city, a relative of his. The result was that Eliezer Ashkenazi was compelled to emigrate again. He went to Prague, but soon returned to Italy, this time to the city of Cremona. In 1578 he arrived in Poland. He was obviously aware that Jewish society in Poland was similar to Italy's Renaissance Jewry. This probably caused him to believe that Poland was the right place for him. He did not err, and Poland's Jewry received him with great respect. Nevertheless, even in Poland he remained the perpetual wanderer. In the few years of his sojourn in Poland he lived in no fewer than three cities, Posen, Gnesen, and Cracow. In the latter city Eliezer Ashkenazi died in 1586. Several decades ago his grave in Cracow's Old Cemetery was discovered.

Rabbi Eliezer Ashkenazi was a versatile scholar. Several of his responsa that have come down to us reveal him as a great halakhist. A scholar who lived about a hundred years later reported that Eliezer Ashkenazi wrote critical notes on the *Beth Yosef* of his teacher Rabbi Joseph Karo. This book, however, is unknown today. Various passages in his writings show that Rabbi Eliezer Ashkenazi also possessed a certain, though limited, degree of knowledge in the secular sciences. He also composed liturgical songs and poems. But in this field he did not achieve much. Rabbi Eliezer Ashkenazi's great literary achievement was in biblical exegesis. A super-commentary that he wrote, according to a certain report, on Moses Nahmanides' commentary on the Pentateuch (Spain, thirteenth century), is unknown. His two commentaries that did survive rate, however, among the most important works of biblical exegesis. The first of the two books is named *Yosef Lekah,* (*May the Book*) *Increase Learning* (comp. Proverbs 1:5) and is a commentary on the Scroll of Esther. Eliezer Ashkenazi wrote it long before he arrived in Poland. It was published in Italy. The second work, however, *Maase Hashem, The Deeds of the Lord,* that surpasses the former by far in importance, was completed in Poland in 1580. Indeed, a large part may have been written there. The book is a remarkable commentary on the historical portions of the Pentateuch, and discusses four subjects: The story of creation till Abraham; from Abraham to the death of Jacob; the story of the Exodus; and from the giving of the Law to the death of Moses. The author makes an effort to convince the reader that it is his duty to believe that all events actually happened in the manner they are recorded in the Torah. The work attained wide acceptance in the scholarly world. It was published almost simultaneously in Venice and in Cracow shortly after its completion. A number of later reprints demonstrate that it remained popular throughout the ages.

XVII.

A completely new phenomenon is the emergence of a literature in Yiddish, and the publication of Yiddish books previously written in other countries. It has been described above how Yiddish steadily became the daily language of the Jews in Eastern Europe. We have also seen how people who did not know the Hebrew language were encouraged to read in Yiddish. Isaac Prostitz, the owner of the printing press in Cracow, believed that there was a great demand for books in Yiddish, and began to publish them. During the last three decades of the century Isaac Prostitz printed more than thirty books in Yiddish. He not only printed books in Yiddish but was also active as a Yiddish translator. He prepared rhymed Yiddish translations of several biblical books, of the Sayings of the Fathers, and of the *selihoth*, penitential prayers recited in the synagogue during the period of the High Holidays.

Most of the books in Yiddish that were published during this period consisted of religious literature, primarily the Bible. Several of the biblical books were published in poetic renditions. Such a translation of the Psalms was published with the idea that the various chapters should be sung with the melody customary for the recital of the *Shemuel Buch, The Book of Samuel,* one of the finest products of the older Yiddish literature. The *Shemuel Buch,* too, was published in Cracow in 1593. Two of the Five Scrolls, the Song of Songs, and the Book of Esther, were published in a version enriched with tales and thoughts from the *midrashim.* Two stories from the Apocrypha were then published in Yiddish too: The Book of Susanna and the Book of Judith. The biblical books in Yiddish were published to serve the unlearned and the women as reading material. Other books such as the Mahazor, the Holiday Prayer Book, the Grace After Meals, the *selihoth,* and various collections of precepts served the practical religious needs of the women. One of the first books published in Yiddish in Cracow (1579) was the *Royzn Gortn, Garden of Roses,* by Moses ben Eliezer, a small treatise of ethics and precepts. Later (1597) the *Seder Mitswoth Nashim, Women's Code of Precepts* was published by a local author, Benjamin Ashkenazi of Grodno, as well as a treatise describing many precepts concerning the Jewish family and the Jewish home in its daily life. According to a legend, the entire *Shulhan Arukh* was also published in Yiddish. The scholars of Vilna, however, were afraid that the women would begin to make decisions for themselves in matters of religion without consulting the rabbis, and they had the edition burnt. This tale is undoubtedly false.

In the Renaissance atmosphere, then prevalent in Polish Jewry, a demand also existed for literature that was not religious in nature, but provided the reader with esthetic pleasure. Yiddish books of this type were indeed published in Poland during this period. They will be described in the following chapter.

The greatest Yiddish work, however, written and published in Poland was a religious book. The *Tseenah Ureenah, Go Forth (O Ye Daughters of Zion) and Gaze* (comp. Song of Songs 3:11) by Jacob ben Isaac became, as is well known, the most popular folk book ever written in Yiddish and it retained its popularity for more than three hundred years. Jacob was born in a learned family about the middle of the sixteenth century and was the author of several books. A glance at the totality of his writings shows that Jacob was the typical popularizer who addressed himself to the masses rather than to the scholars. His only book in Hebrew *Shoresh Yaakov, The Root of Jacob,* is an alphabetically arranged index to the sources of the precepts contained in the Yoreh Deah section of the *Shulhan Arukh.* His three books in Yiddish were especially intended for the wide public. In *Melits Yosher, Preacher of Uprightness* (comp. Job 33:23), he collected from various books interesting comments on many passages of the Pentateuch. With this book Jacob gave those who were unable to listen to a preacher, especially Jews living in the villages, an opportunity to read beautiful explanations of sections of the Pentateuch. The book, however, did not gain the popularity its author hoped for. Obviously the printed comment could not compete with the living word of the preacher.

More successful was his book *Hamaggid, The Preacher,* which is a Yiddish commentary on the Prophets and Hagiographa (except Chronicles), also collected from the writings of the classical commentators. This book was intended as a sort of reference volume for self-taught persons to aid them in the study of the Prophets. The author hoped that this book would help its readers to attain an appreciable degree of learning. The book was published, indeed, many times in Poland, Bohemia, and Germany. The greatest success, however, was attained by Jacob ben Isaac's *Tseenah Ureenah.* In the three hundred and fifty years that have passed since the book was written, it has been printed countless times. About one hundred and thirty editions are known to bibliographers. There is no doubt, too, that many other editions were published of which no trace has remained. The book was so universally and ardently read that most of its copies were simply reduced to dust in the hands of its readers. Even in our own times the book was very popular wherever the Jewish masses spoke and read Yiddish. Parts of it were at different times translated into Latin, French, and German.

What was it that made this folk-book so immensely popular?

To begin with, it was a wondrous paraphrase of the Pentateuch, the Haftarahs, and the Five Scrolls. It was also a wonderful, hearty, and poetical re-telling of the stories of the Pentateuch. The biblical stories are interwoven with many legends, parables, and anecdotes from the vast treasures of the Talmud and the Midrash. The book is written in a tender, rhythmic language and in an intimate popular vein. Moral admonitions are here coupled with fantastic tales, and a spirit of sincere and serene piety hovers over its pages. The sublime content and the melodious prose, together with a touching simplicity, captivated the hearts of generations of Jewish mothers and daughters to whom the *Tseenah Ureenah* became a living spring of faith and religious bliss. During the long Friday evenings in the winter, and in the sunny Sabbath afternoons of summer, every Jewish mother would sit surrounded by her daughters and read to them the breathtaking stories of the Humash in the sweet language of the *Tseenah Ureenah*. These stories gave them consolation and courage in hard times and strengthened their morale. Together with the works of the great scholars, the *Tseenah Ureenah* is a monument of the high spiritual and cultural progress that East European Jewry experienced in those times.

XVIII.

The cultural phenomena of the last decades of the sixteenth century and the early seventeenth century that we have described so far belong to the realm of the religious life. True, this was an epoch of outspoken intellectualism, with the influence and tendencies of the Renaissance prominently evident. Basically, however, the Polish Jew of those times was a pious man for whom moral behavior and the service of God were the highest ideals. This is borne out by the fact that about one-third of the Hebrew and Yiddish books published in Poland during this epoch concerned religion and prayer. It is worth noting that some of the most important commentaries on the prayer book were written in this epoch in Poland.

The frequently mentioned Rabbi Nathan Shapiro, one of the prominent scholars of the time, was the author of a commentary on the *zemiroth shel Shabbath,* the Sabbath (meal) hymns, and on the Grace after Meals. He was also the author of a commentary on the Mahazor, the Holiday Prayer Book. Other works of a similar nature were written by some of his younger contemporaries. The commentary on the prayer book of Isaiah Horovitz, *Shaar Hashamaim, Gate of Heaven,* attained great fame. Its author included in his commentary many thoughts and customs of the kabbalists. A large number of special prayers were written in times of epidemics and other calamities. Other poems mourned victims of the recurring fires in the crowded Jewish streets or recorded the memory and heroism of Jews who died for the sanctification of the Name of God. Most of these liturgical poems do not possess much aesthetic beauty. But the hearty and serene spirit in which their authors composed them ultimately paved the way for many of them to be incorporated into the various regional or universal orders of Jewish prayer.

Besides these authors and commentators, there were two scholars of note, both of the city of Przemysl, who composed outstanding works about prayer and the service of God, Sabbatai the Scribe and the already mentioned Moses the Dead. Sabbatai's profession, as his name shows, was to prepare phylacteries, Torah Scrolls, and other ritual documents. In addition, he was a great Hebrew grammarian, possibly the most outstanding in East Europe during those times. The profession of scribe, whose task was to painstakingly prepare copies of holy texts, and his interest in grammar made him very alert to the accuracy of literary documents. As pointed out above, there was also a general predilection for textual criticism. All this induced Sabbatai to embark upon a specific task: to scrutinize the texts of the various prayers of the Siddur with the view of establishing the correct text. He thought that great damage might be caused by letting little children study the prayers from erroneous texts. He approached his work with scholarly methodology, and was very careful not to suggest corrections for which no corroborative evidence was available in the writings of earlier and contemporary authorities. He drew his material from the Talmud and its main commentaries, Rashi and the Tosafoth, as well as from nearly forty other works. In addition, he collected many old manuscripts of the Mahazor and the Siddur to verify the correctness of the liturgical texts. After completing this basic research project, Sabbatai wrote a comprehensive commentary on the Siddur, the mere Introduction to which is almost a book in itself. The Siddur as corrected by Rabbi Sabbatai the Scribe was reprinted many times. The commentary, however, remained unpublished. Only at the beginning of our century the Introduction to it was published by Abraham Berliner, himself an expert in the history and text of the Siddur.

As already indicated, Sabbatai's close friend was a great scholar and fine author with the bizarre name of Moses the Dead. The contemporary scholarly world did not reconcile itself to this strange name and preferred to call him Moses, the Living Man. He was the son of a certain Abraham, who died as a martyr. Moses was one of the foremost students of Rabbi Solomon Luria. His writings are permeated with stories about his great teacher's religious life. He served as rabbi and rosh yeshivah in Belz and in Przemysl, both important communities in southeastern Poland. For reasons unknown to us Rabbi Moses was compelled to leave Belz. From there he went to Vladimir Volinsk, where his father-in-law was a citizen with the reputation of a magnanimous philanthropist. Obviously Moses hoped that the father-in-law would establish a yeshivah for him. His great desire was to be surrounded by pupils as he had been during his stay in Belz. His hope seems not to have been fulfilled, and so he decided to become an author. As there was no opportunity for him to teach, he thought, people would at least study his books.

The work that he wrote is named *Matte Mosheh, Moses' Rod,* probably to stress the fact that the book was a support and consolation to him. It is a book which describes the many laws and religious folkways by which a good Jew should live. It is divided into three parts: The Pillar of Torah, The Pillar of Service, and The Pillar of Charity. This was in accordance with Sayings of the Fathers, Chapter 1: "By three things is the world sustained, by the Law, by the (Temple) Service, and by the Deeds of Loving-Kindness." In the first part we find a presentation of the importance of the study of Torah and of the duty to honor the scholars. The scholars in turn are advised how to best organize their study and how to behave in a manner befitting them. The third part of the book discusses the *mitswah* of charity in its various forms. This part is one great, passionate plea for justice and charity. The second part, by far the largest, is given to a systematic presentation of the rules concerning the prayers, the Sabbath, the holidays, and all the other areas of the religious conduct of the individual. The discussion of the texts of various prayers is accompanied by a presentation of the reasons for their recital. Being a child of his time, he corrected here and there the texts of the prayers. But this was far less important to him than to his friend Rabbi Sabbatai the Scribe.

From a literary point of view, the *Matte Mosheh* is unusually well written. Its style is one of beauty and clarity. The text is made exceptionally vivid by the many passages which the erudite writer quotes from books by a variety of authors. The author manifests his literary talent when he describes various areas of the religious law in rhymed prose. His skill is also evident when he, for example, explains the reason for the drinking of four cups of wine at the Passover Seder in four ways: the simple expositional way, the allegorical way of the sages, the kabbalistic way, and the way of logical reasoning. The material used by the author is distributed truly systematically; and all of this is enveloped in a sincere enthusiasm for *yiddishkeit* that made a great impression on the pious reader three hundred years ago and continues to impress today's reader. The book was first published in Cracow during the author's lifetime and was reprinted early in the seventeenth century in Germany. It was published again in Poland during the nineteenth century; a photostatic reprint was recently issued.

CHAPTER SIX

THE LIBERAL ARTS AND OTHER DISCIPLINES

I.

The sixteenth century was a period when the cultural and scholarly life of Poland flourished. The spirit of the Renaissance, and even more that of humanism, penetrated many circles of society. Large numbers of young Poles studied at the universities of Germany and Italy, wherefrom they returned with a deep interest in knowledge and in research. This cultural blossoming reached a peak during the reign of the last Yagiellonian, Sigismund August (1548–1572).

As we have seen, the Jewish society of Poland, too, had direct contact with Italy's Jewish community and was strongly influenced by it. Humanistic influences and interests also streamed into the Jewish quarters from neighboring Christian society. Rabbi Ephraim Lunchits explicitly states that social relations existed between the higher strata of the Jewish population and Christians.

The humanistic interest in the sciences and in literature among the Jews was, however, strongly limited by the study of the Talmud and the Halakhah, which imposed a decisive imprint upon all areas of life. To be sure, energetic efforts were made to satisfy the interest in areas of knowledge other than Talmud. Nonetheless, the sciences in Jewish society were assigned a lesser rank.

As in other times and in other countries, Poland's Jewish spiritual leadership of the sixteenth century seriously discussed the problem of whether it should be permissible to study the sciences and if so, to what degree. The admirers of the sciences

136

used the well-known argument that the Gentile neighbors would respect the Jewish people more if they would cultivate the sciences. An anonymous scholar in Posen, who in 1559 conducted a valiant fight in defense of Maimonides and of philosophy in general, relates that the Talmudic and sermonic literature, the two main areas of Jewish intellectual endeavor, had become a matter for derision by the Gentiles. He was convinced that an increased preoccupation with non-Jewish disciplines would also put the Talmud in a better light.

The friendly attitude of certain other scholars toward the sciences stemmed from a more positive approach. Rabbi Matathiah Delakrut explicitly tells us that he translated the French medieval book *Image du Monde, Image of the World,* which he named in Hebrew *Tsel Haolam,* because he envied the non-Jewish world for having such a fine work on the sciences. Isaac of Troki, the religious polemicist, had a deep appreciation of the learning of the Gentiles, and being a true humanist, he recognized its educational and moral values. Rabbi Mordecai Yaffe was also obviously in favor of the study of the various disciplines when he suggested that whereas it is hard to reach all the secrets of the Torah because of its divine character, it is theoretically possible to attain the knowledge of the sciences because they are of human origin. He, too, was of the opinion that preoccupation with the sciences would evoke Gentile respect for the Jews.

The main dispute, however, centered around the question of whether it is permissible to study the sciences, and whether a Jew has the right to divert part of his time from the study of Torah to other intellectual endeavors. In the middle of the century, Rabbi Moses Isserles had discussed the question and had given clear permission for one to study the sciences on certain conditions. Moreover, even Rabbi Solomon Luria, who criticized Moses Isserles and his pupils for their interest in the sciences, was himself well-versed in them and, not without pride, professed his knowledge of philosophy. Indeed, later in the century we find no one except the rabbi of Posen, Aaron —if what his opponent tells us about him is true—opposing the sciences as a matter of principle. The only reservation made by Rabbi Mordecai Yaffe, for example, refers to the *sifre minin,* the books of the heretics (comp. tractates Baba Kama 83a and Menahoth 99b). Moses Isserles declared that the opposition of the sages to "Greek wisdom" refers to metaphysics, but not to the sciences. He also believed that the ban on the study of philosophy issued by the great religious leader of Spanish Jewry, Rabbi Solomon ibn Adreth (1235–1310), was directed solely against those who neglected the study of the Torah. Moses Isserles was therefore of the opinion—and so were Rabbi Mordecai Yaffe and Rabbi Moses the Dead—that after a Jew had acquired a proper knowledge of the Torah, especially in the area of *issur weheter,* i.e., what is prohibited and what is permitted, he may study the sciences when an opportunity presents itself. Rabbi Moses Isserles used to study philosophy on the Sabbath, on holidays, and at the time when people "take a walk," i.e., in his leisure. The same approach also motivated him to permit, in opposition to a decision in the *Shulhan Arukh,* the reading of books of historical content on the Sabbath. His attitude toward the natural sciences, from which he used to derive conclusions in matters of the religious law, was even more friendly. The natural sciences, and especially medicine, were utilized even by Rabbi Solomon Luria to make decisions in matters of Halakhah.

The great scholars of the next generation went still further. They considered the sciences to be an ancillary discipline to the study of Talmud. Rabbi Samuel Edels and Rabbi Ephraim Lunchits both agreed that the sciences are a sort of introduction to the Torah. Rabbi Samuel says that in the way *soleth,* fine flour meal, is used to make bread, so the sciences can be used for the understanding of the Torah. Ephraim Lunchits expressed the same thought with more clarity, saying that without the knowledge of mathematics, physics, and astronomy the Torah cannot be properly understood. Rabbi Levi ben Bezalel, in turn, says somewhat picturesquely that the sciences are "a ladder" which one has to climb to attain the correct understanding of the Torah.

A careful analysis of the writings of the halakhists and of the preachers shows that most of them had, indeed, acquired a considerable amount of knowledge in the non-Talmudic disciplines. We will later describe Polish Jewry's achievements in the arts and sciences in detail. Suffice to note here that its knowledge in the various areas was of a much wider range than its literary production in these fields. In view of this fact the conclusion has to be reached that Polish Jewry's thirst for knowledge in the sciences was, to a great measure, satisfied by reading the rich Hebrew scientific literature produced by Spanish Jewry as well as similar books in the Polish language. The validity of this conclusion is attested to by the fact that practically all of the many works that Manoah Hendel wrote in the field of the sciences remained unpublished. The desire for knowledge could no doubt be satisfied through books written elsewhere and in earlier times.

In 1807, Tadeusz Czacki, a Polish scholar of note, published an interesting book about the Jews of his country. In this book the author printed a document he found in one of the state archives. It contains an appeal to the Jewish people by Jewish leaders to study the sciences. Czacki believed that the document dated back to the first half of the sixteenth century. Some Jewish historians today are of the opinion that this appeal is of a much later origin and was probably issued late in the eighteenth century when many efforts were made in Poland to improve the political, economic, and cultural conditions of the Jewish population. Still, when one delves deeply into the literature of Poland's Jewry of the sixteenth century, and realizes how warm the attitude toward the sciences was, one begins to think that this appeal perhaps does stem from those remote times. The appeal stresses, in accordance with the attitude of Rabbi Moses Isserles and of the sages who lived at the turn of the century, the fact that a Jew should not content himself solely with the study of Torah but should rather strive to attain knowledge in other fields. If the "Fruit of the Paradise" (the Torah) is so good, are we not, urges the appeal, permitted to eat simple apples (the secular sciences)? The document goes on to show how in former ages the sciences achieved a high status among the Jewish people, and it requests that the Jews should acquire secular knowledge and, by doing so, become useful to the king and to the nobility. The appeal closes with a statement that sounds like a perfect echo of the Renaissance: "The king considers all his subjects like a great forest (full of trees) . . . nobody asks of what seed the most beautiful tree sprouts. Why then should not from us grow out among the thorns a beautiful tree?"

· Whether this interesting appeal stems from the sixteenth century or not, it is clear that a great many of the Polish Jews of the sixteenth century, besides their unusual involvement in the study of the Talmud also cultivated other areas of knowledge, Jewish as well as general.

II.

A good example is the attitude of the Polish Jews to the study of the Hebrew language and its grammar. There were scholars who did not care at all for the rules of grammar. Even a scholar of Rabbi Moses Isserles' magnitude wrote in a style full of grammatical errors. When the disciplined humanist Rabbi Solomon Luria reproached him for this, Isserles retorted (with reference to the Hebrew word *dikduk,* grammar), that his complaints were *dikduke aniyuth,* pedantry. He neglected grammar, says Isserles, because he was totally concerned with *what* he said rather than with *how* he said it. He admitted, in conclusion, that he had never studied Hebrew grammar. This weakness plagued most of Poland's Jewish scholars and evoked derision from their Italian contemporaries. Rabbi Azariah dei Rossi, one of the greatest humanists, was amazed by the poor style in which Isserles' philosophical work *Torath Haolah* was written. Another Italian rabbi-author discussed this problem at a later time and opined that Rabbi Jacob Pollack, the founding father of Poland's Talmudic studies, refrained from literary activity because he did not possess the ability to write proper Hebrew.

In later times, too, Poland's Jewish scholars were not yet convinced that grammar was an important field of study. Even as colorful a personality as Meir of Lublin belonged to this group. Contemporaries report that the cantors who chanted the prayers in the synagogues pronounced Hebrew words incorrectly. This lax and indifferent attitude toward language and its laws was deeply rooted in the soul of the Polish Jew. Down to our own times the Polish Jew believed that it was important *what* one says rather than *how* one says it. Scholars could nevertheless be found among the Polish Jews at that time who began to stress the importance of the study of grammar. Sabbatai the Scribe, author of the excellent commentary to the prayer book, criticized Rabbi Meir of Lublin for his indifferent attitude toward grammar and proved the duty to study it in an especially composed pamphlet. Isaiah Horovitz and Mordecai Yaffe lent support to the idea and made explicit demands that the study of grammar should be an integral part of the curriculum of the *heder,* the Jewish elementary school. There was also a number of scholars who, though they did not participate in the discussion of the virtues of grammar, possessed considerable knowledge of the Hebrew language. That Moses the Dead knew Hebrew grammar is not astonishing. He was, after all, a devoted pupil of Rabbi Solomon Luria. Rabbi Nathan Shapiro of Grodno was versed in the works of some of the medieval grammarians. Other authors, too, demonstrated their knowledge of Hebrew grammar. In various sources *medakdekim,* grammarians, are mentioned, showing that there were scholars who specialized in grammar. Deeply interested in this subject was David the Preacher. It will be recalled that when he planned to establish an "academy" he considered offering a special course in grammar for the *melamdim,* the elementary school teachers. Sabbatai the Scribe was even more involved in the study of Hebrew grammar. There was hardly a book in this area that he had not studied for the composition of his great commentary on the Jewish Prayer Book. In fact, his greatest achievements in this commentary were made possible by his unusual knowledge of grammar. The contemporaries, and also later writers, call him *hamedakdek hagadol,* the great grammarian. The Council of the Four Provinces in its approbation of the commentary to the Prayer Book, too, stressed the author's knowledge of Hebrew grammar.

The universal interest in the study of the Halakhah did not leave enough ground for the development of a grammatical literature of true importance. Among more than two hundred books published in this period in Cracow and Lublin, only a negligible number is in the area of Hebrew grammar. Also, the books that were written in Poland in this area show little originality. They all are mainly commentaries on the works of the medieval Spanish and Provençal Hebrew grammarians. Manoah Hendel, the popularizer, wrote commentaries on three of them. Curiously, the "great grammarian" himself wrote two such commentaries, to the *Mahalakh Shevile Hadaath, A Journey on the Pathways of Knowledge,* by Moses Kimhi (second half of the twelfth century), and to the *Mikhlol, (The Book of Perfection)* of his younger brother David, known as Radak. This last commentary was not published and Sabbatai almost lost it to a plagiarist who had copied the work and had begun to publicize it as his own. Sabbatai's main contribution lies in the fact that he described all the rules of Hebrew grammar in the introduction to his Prayer Book, and made it easily accessible to the average Jew in this manner. The dissemination of the knowledge of *dikduk* (grammar) was best achieved through a concise textbook *Em Hayeled, The Mother of the Child,* written by an immigrant teacher from Italy, Joseph Halpern, who lived in Posen. His method of teaching proved to be so successful that even small children quickly acquired a knowledge of grammar. The explanations of the various rules are given in this textbook in Yiddish. The book was published at the end of the century simultaneously in Prague and in Cracow with the warm recommendation of Rabbi Mordecai Yaffe.

The actual knowledge of the Hebrew language and the ability to write it far surpassed the interest in *dikduk.* This ability was simply acquired through the perennial study of the old Hebrew texts. In Poland there was always a number of people who wrote Hebrew in an excellent style. The polemical work *Hizzuk Emunah, Strengthening of the Faith,* by Isaac of Troki is written in a beautiful Hebrew style. Moses the Dead, Isaiah Horovitz, and David the Preacher, all wrote a beautiful Hebrew; the last mentioned also wrote Aramaic in a fine style. The scholars who were versed in the philosophical literature of the Middle Ages acquired from it the ability to write the language of the scholars. People who had a good Hebrew style at their command usually served as secretaries of the Jewish communal institutions. Hebrew was the official language of the communal chancery, that usually wanted its documents issued in a correct Hebrew style. For example, Joseph, who was the scribe of the rabbinic court in Posen at the turn of the century, possessed a fine Hebrew style. He is the author of a liturgical poem describing the martyrdom of two brothers of the town of Gombin.

It is noteworthy that a certain interest in Hebrew manifested itself also among the Christians, especially in Protestant circles. Among them, however, knowledge of the holy tongue was very rare and remained far behind the great Hebrew linguistic interest of the German and Italian Christian humanists. All that we know is that several Latin books were published that dealt with the Hebrew language. Only the famous religious reformer Simon Budny, and the magnate Jan Koniecpolski, and perhaps two or three other men, had acquired a knowledge of the Hebrew language to a considerable degree.

III.

The study of the Prophets and Hagiographa was not too popular either. The Pentateuch was, of course, studied by every Jew. School children studied the weekly portion of the Pentateuch year after year. Adults also fulfilled the *mitswah* of reading the weekly portions every Sabbath. In the yeshivahs, however, with their emphasis on the study of the Talmud and the jurisprudence literature, the study of the Bible was neglected. Successful study of Jewish legal literature demanded, indeed, the undivided devotion of the student. Consequently, the yeshivah left little time for other subjects. In addition, the study of Talmud, which required considerable intellectual effort, made the simple study of the Bible appear as an occupation suitable for children and uneducated adults. The delusion was also widespread that since countless verses of the Prophets and Hagiographa are quoted in the Talmud and in the *midrashim,* the student of Talmud was automatically bound to achieve a knowledge of the Bible.

The neglectful attitude toward the study of the Prophets rarely became explicit opposition. Though Rabbi Solomon Luria's pupil believed that only the study of the Talmud would hasten the coming of the Messiah, and that preoccupation with the Bible would not strengthen piety, such opinions were rare. In most cases the Bible was neglected much in the way the scholars neglected the study of grammar. It is interesting that opponents of the Pilpul such as Rabbi Levi ben Bezalel and Rabbi Isaiah Horovitz voiced the explicit demand that more attention should be directed to the study of the Bible. The anonymous scholar who so ardently defended the study of philosophy in Posen was also explicitly in favor of the study of the Bible. The argument became more heated whenever the study of the Bible in the curriculum of the elementary school (*heder*) came up for discussion.

A perusal of the contemporary literature shows that despite the neglectful attitude, knowledge of the Holy Writ was widespread. The above-mentioned opponent of the study of Bible admits that there were *baale krayan,* experts in the Scriptures, i.e., men whose fame as scholars rested on their knowledge of the Bible. He also mentions that he personally knew an old man whose knowledge of the Bible was unusual. The works of the preachers, of course, overflow with biblical passages. A quick glimpse at the writings of Rabbi Ephraim Lunchits convinces one that he was no less versed in the Bible than in the Talmud. We get the same impression when we read Rabbi Moses Isserles' *Torath Haolah,* with its numerous quotations not only from the Pentateuch but also from the Prophets and Hagiographa. Among the less educated laity the Psalms were well known, both because so many of them are part of the Prayer Book and because of the ever-spreading custom of reciting them daily in especially established groups. The sources tell us that this custom was a recent innovation. Rabbi Isaiah Horovitz, delighted with this development as he was, still had to admit to himself that these groups were interested in reciting the Psalms rather than in studying them. He was one of the first to voice his concern about this.

The literary production of the epoch in the area of biblical exegesis was very meager. It goes without saying that the collections of sermons contained commentaries on many biblical verses, both of the standard and allegorical types. Homilies, are not, however, systematically organized commentaries that can be used as an aid to the study of the Prophets or Hagiographa. Such systematic commentaries were rare because of the limited interest in the study of the Prophets and Hagiographa, and also because it was difficult to compose truly original works in this area. Indeed, we recall that Rabbi Ephraim Lunchits originally intended to devote himself to this field, but quickly realized that almost all of his explanations already had been suggested in former biblical commentaries.

An enumeration of the contemporary biblical commentaries reveals how few they were. Moses Isserles' allegorical treatise on the Scroll of Esther, *Mehir Yayin,* can hardly be considered a commentary, as it is actually a philosophical essay. Of a similar nature was probably his commentary on the Song of Songs which he mentions in *Torath Haolah.* Most of the works of Rabbi Ephraim Lunchits cannot be considered biblical commentaries since the homiletical element predominates. Only Naphtali Altschuler's commentary on the Prophets and Hagiographa *Ayyalah Sheluhah, The Hind Let Loose* (comp. Genesis 49:21), was of practical significance. The book is an anthology of good explanations selected from many commentaries.

It is supplemented by a dictionary that gives the Yiddish translation of uncommon words. A similar popular commentary on the entire Bible was written by Manoah Hendel. Unfortunately, this book remained unpublished like most of his other works. So the biblical commentary, probably the most important written in this epoch, remained unknown.

IV.

The lack of real interest in the study of *dikduk* and of the Bible is probably the main factor that prevented the Polish Jewry of that time from producing a Hebrew poetry or secular prose of any consequence. A perusal of the source material proves that Polish-Jewish authors did write poems and that their number is impressive. With few exceptions these, however, were occasional poems that lack originality and imagination. Even such a thinker and excellent writer as Ephraim Lunchits produced only mediocre poems such as the one printed at the end of his *Oleloth Ephraim*.

A certain interest in poetical forms can be seen in the predilection of scholars for rhymed prose. Almost all of them included larger or smaller specimens of rhymed prose in their halakhic works. In this fashion Meir of Lublin wrote many of his responsa, and so did Rabbi Benjamin Solnik, as evidenced in his work *Maseath Binyamin, Benjamin's Portion* (comp. Genesis 43:34). Rhymed prose was also the form in which prefaces to Hebrew books were commonly written. In this manner, for example, introductions to Mordecai Yaffe's *Levushim,* to the polemical work *Hizzuk Emunah,* and to Nathan Shapiro's *Mevo Shearim* were composed. The latter's rhymed prose is superior to that produced by any other contemporary writer in Poland.

Other authors, e.g., Moses the Dead, composed considerable parts of their works in rhymed prose. Of special interest are the rhymed collections of religious laws which were fashionable at that time. Rabbi Solomon Luria presented the Passover ritual in rhymed prose, and Rabbi Isaac Hayes followed his example. Moses the Dead, too, presented the 613 precepts in this fashion. All of these authors probably wanted to achieve a double goal: to employ a talent they knew that they possessed, and at the same time to enable the reader to more easily remember the numerous laws and precepts. The bilingual folkbook *Sam Hayim, Elixir,* by Abraham the Druggist, mentioned above many times, was also composed in rhymed prose. Some samples of bizarre literary forms also made their appearance in Poland. Such is the introduction to the Lublin Mishnah edition published towards the end of the century. Like similar Provençal and Italian poems, the introduction was made up of three hundred words, each of which began with the letter *mem,* which is also the first letter of the word "Mishnah."

Almost all the poetry that was composed in Poland at that time can be divided into three groups: songs and hymns in honor of the Sabbath and the holidays; occasional poems written in honor of an author or his book, and usually printed in the book; and poems of mourning which either gave expression to the feelings of the people in moments of suffering and disaster, or memorialized contemporary martyrs who died for the sanctification of the Name of God.

Even the authors who showed some interest in composing prayers and hymns wrote very little. Rabbi Solomon Luria was the author of thirteen poems in honor of the Sabbath. A number of prayers and hymns was written by Rabbi Eliezer Ashkenazi, the learned immigrant from the Near East. These poems were published in Cracow about five years after their author's arrival in Poland, and we may therefore assume that he composed them there. Some prayers were composed by other contemporary rabbis. Several prayers written by Rabbi Isaiah Horovitz are included in his great work.

Isaiah Horovitz, to whom every part of the Jewish prayer book was very dear, was an admirer of the *piyutim,* the supplemental prayers found in the various prayer books. He was not in favor of correcting their texts. Obviously, the tendency to correct and improve earlier texts, which was so prevalent in the Rabbinic literature of the times, also concentrated on the *piyu-*

tim. From this we can infer that there was more than casual interest in this type of literature, at least among the scholars. A more realistic attitude to the *piyutim* was expressed by Rabbi Ephraim Lunchits. He argued that they were built too much on *midrashic* material and were unintelligible to the average worshipper, whose familiarity with the *midrashim* was only superficial.

Religious poems of a more contemporary character were the *selihoth* and *kinoth,* that is to say, penitential prayers and dirges composed to commemorate various tragic events. Many such poems were composed, for example, after a terrible fire in Posen in 1590 took the lives of fifteen people and destroyed more than seventy Torah scrolls. Many more *kinoth* were composed to eulogize two brothers from the town of Gombin who were burned at the stake in Warsaw in 1596 because of an accusation that they stole the holy wafer. Some of the most prominent rabbis of Poland were among the authors of these *kinoth.* Rabbi Mordecai Yaffe, who at the time was rabbi of Posen, commissioned the above-mentioned communal secretary, Joseph ben Solomon, to compose such a *kinah.* He made the poem part of the *Musaf* service of the Day of Atonement and had it especially printed to make it possible for many other communities to commemorate the martyrdom of the brothers. In Cracow these martyrs were commemorated in a prayer written in their honor by Rabbi Moses Mordecai Margalith, a local scholar.

Rabbi Shabbetai the Scribe of Przemysl, the author of the great commentary on the Siddur, likewise composed a poem in honor of a local martyr in 1630. The poem became part of the worship of a special fast day held annually in memory of the martyr. Although this poem, too, is a mere description of the tragic event, it is nevertheless of a somewhat higher literary quality. To be sure, Rabbi Shabbetai cannot be considered a true poet. Yet, his unusual familiarity with the world of prayer, and with the grammar of the holy tongue, added much beauty to his verses and made his rhymes smoother than those of most other *kinoth* writers.

In summing up the poor record of Hebrew poetry, it should be noted that quite a number of poems appear at the beginning or the end of many books that were printed in Poland during this period. Sometimes the author of the book is also the author of the poems, such as those published by Rabbi Mordecai Yaffe and Rabbi Isaiah Horovitz in their works. Sometimes, instead, the rhymester is a friend or admirer of the author of the book, as is the case with the poem printed at the end of Rabbi Moses Isserles' *Torath Haolah.* From time to time such a poem was even written by the printer or the proofreader of the work. Most of these poems have, of course, little if any literary value.

It is hard to explain why Hebrew poetry in Poland was so poor at a time when Polish literature was experiencing a period of unusual greatness, with poets of the magnitude of Jan Kochanowski. The only plausible explanation may again lie in the fact that Jewish intellectual life was so exclusively dominated by the study of the Talmud, that most other spiritual activities were *eo ipso* eliminated. The fact that Yiddish poetry stood on a much higher level seems to support this explanation. It seems that the circles that remained outside the mainstream of Torah learning (the women and the uneducated), and were dependent on the Yiddish language in their intellectual pursuits, did manifest a yearning for true poetry. It should be noted that in this period two new editions of the *Shmuel Buch* were published in Cracow. In this work, written in verse, a medieval Yiddish author retells the story contained in the biblical book of Samuel. It is one of the outstanding works of the older Yiddish literature. That the average Yiddish-reading Jew of that time manifested a demand for this book is a testimony to his good literary taste. In that period in Cracow there also appeared Yiddish translations in verse of various other biblical books. A contemporary Polish-Jewish author, Jacob Koppelman, also translated in verse the famous collection of stories *Mishle Shualim, Fox Fables* by Berechiah Hanakdan. This beautiful book, written for the purpose of teaching men the good way of life through stories from the lives of the animals, greatly enriched the library of the Polish Jew who read in Yiddish.

The Polish Jew of that time also looked for reading material that would entertain him rather than lift him spiritually. Isaac Prostitz, the Cracow printer who published the Yiddish translations of the various Biblical books, tells us that he was proud of the fact that he was publishing the Holy Writ, while other printers were publishing books whose sole purpose was to entertain the reader. As we recall, Rabbi Moses Isserles permitted the reading of "secular stories on wars" if they were written in the Hebrew language. The demand for such secular literature was amply manifested by the publication of a Yiddish translation of the famous German chivalry poem *Dietrich von Bern*. Curiously, its publisher was Isaac Prostitz himself. The publisher termed the poem "a beautiful song" and promised that it would serve as excellent entertainment.

V.

The knowledge of languages seems to have been fairly widespread among Poland's Jews. At the beginning of the sixteenth century the average Gentile knew only one language, his native Polish tongue. In the course of the century, however, conditions developed that greatly increased the knowledge of foreign languages among the population. Within Jewish society the knowledge of foreign languages was an even more common phenomenon. Poland's Jewish community continued to grow as the result of immigration from Germany and Bohemia. The new arrivals, of course, brought with them a knowledge of German, and to a lesser degree, Czech. No doubt, many Jews knew Polish and Ukrainian, the languages of the two parts of the Commonwealth. The preacher Ephraim Lunchits reports that wealthy Jews had social intercourse with Gentiles. We have, of course, to assume that they conversed in Polish. In 1542, Bishop Gamrat of Cracow demanded that Jewish students be excluded from Polish schools. This indicates that Jewish students did attend Polish schools although their number was probably limited. Jews who lived in the territories of the Lithuanian Grand Duchy understood White Russian and Ukrainian, and some of them communicated in these languages in the early seventeenth century. Among the scholars, Rabbi Meir of Lublin knew Polish and Rabbi Solomon Luria knew both Polish and Ukrainian. The latter had lived in both parts of the Commonwealth and therefore mastered both languages. We will have to assume the same with regard to many other scholars who successively held rabbinic positions in the western and eastern regions of the Kingdom. Isaac of Troki, author of *Hizzuk Emunah,* knew the Polish language very well and was acquainted with its literature. The manner in which he quoted the New Testament in his work indicates that he read it in the Polish language. The sources regrettably fail to inform us whether the Jews who lived in the purely Lithuanian regions, such as Samogitia, knew Lithuanian, the tongue of the native population.

The knowledge of languages other than those spoken in Poland was, of course, less common. Immigrants from Italy, as well as Polish Jews who spent some time there (Rabbis Matathiah Delakrut and Mordecai Yaffe, and young men who studied medicine in Padua), naturally acquired a knowledge of Italian. The knowledge of Latin was found mainly among the physicians, and primarily among those who had studied in Padua. An author of the late sixteenth century mentions a Jew who was versed in the Arabic language.

VI.

In the sciences and mathematical disciplines, the Polish Jews were completely dependent on the Sephardic-Hebrew scientific literature, as well as on books in Polish and in German. Among the two hundred Hebrew books printed during this period in Poland, only a few belong to the area of the sciences. The cosmography *Tsel Haolam, Image of the World,* which

Matathiah Delakrut translated shortly before his return from Italy to Poland, was not printed before the eighteenth century, and even then not in Poland. On the other hand, however, we find a considerable amount of mathematical and scientific knowledge in the Polish-Jewish literature of the epoch. One can see from the writings of Rabbi Moses Isserles that his knowledge of the sciences was considerable, and enabled him to form for himself a fairly adequate view of nature and of the universe. He, indeed, quoted the various Hebrew scientific works written in Spain countless times. It is possible that the lack of new, locally written works motivated him to encourage his Bohemian student David Gans to compose a book on astronomy and climatology. Rabbi Ephraim Lunchits, who lived much later, was convinced that it was possible for the Jew in Poland to study the sciences. He suggested that a man should first study the natural sciences "in order to learn and achieve the knowledge of natural phenomena in this world." Following this, one should study cosmography, and only then proceed to the study of "what is beyond this world."

The knowledge of botany and zoology, as presented in the Polish-Jewish literature of the time, is quite limited. The mathematical sciences, however, aroused real interest among the Polish-Jewish scholars. Almost all great Talmudic teachers used mathematics to interpret many passages in the Talmud and its main commentaries. In his writings Rabbi Moses Isserles discussed various mathematical problems and was aware of the connection between mathematics and music. We also find mathematical observations in the writings of Rabbi Mordecai Yaffe and Rabbi Samuel Edels. The latter considered this discipline to be a "prerequisite" to the study of Torah.

The Talmudic scholars had specific opportunities to make use of their knowledge of geometry in their efforts to interpret certain parts of the tractates of Sabbath and Erubin ("The Fusion of Sabbath Limits"). We find, indeed, many geometrical figures in Manoah Hendel's *Hokhmath Manoah* and in the commentary of Rabbi Samuel Edels. In the latter such figures are abundant even with regard to Talmudic passages where neither Rashi nor the Tosafists had drawn such. Obviously, Samuel Edels drew these figures on his own initiative. The greatest number of geometrical figures is found in Rabbi Solomon Luria's *Hokhmath Shelomoh*, in the section Erubin. Curiously, it is quite possible that Solomon Luria, who manifested a less friendly attitude to the sciences than other Polish rabbis, was better versed in the sciences than all his colleagues.

The interest in mathematics described above did not produce a mathematical literature. Only two authors wrote anything in this area, but only the work of one of them appeared in print. Jacob Koppelman of Brzesc Kujawski, whom we shall meet later as the author of a commentary on Joseph Albo's philosophical work *Sefer Haikkarim, (The Book of Root Principles)*, was very much interested in mathematics. This becomes obvious when reading his commentary on Albo. In addition, Koppelman wrote the treatise *Omek Halakhah, The Depth of the Law*, which is a commentary on mathematical passages in the Talmud. The treatise, published in Cracow in the 1590's, was later republished in Amsterdam.

Another author of mathematical works was Manoah Hendel, the great popularizer. He composed a commentary on the *Sefer Hamispar, Book of Mathematics,* of Elijah Mizrahi, the famous chief rabbi of Turkey, and a commentary on seven sections of one of Euclid's works, probably the *Book of Elements*. Both of these commentaries contain many explanations of mathematical passages in the Talmud. These two books shared the fate of Manoah Hendel's other works; they were never printed.

Polish Jewry manifested its most genuine interest in the sciences during this period in the field of astronomy. If credence can be given to a certain Latin source, Polish Jews were preoccupied with astronomy already in the early years of the sixteenth century. Their interest in astronomy had various roots. To begin with, the belief in astrology, very popular among the men of the Renaissance, was also widespread among the Polish Jews. This, naturally, prompted the average man to acquire a certain knowledge of the stars. The philosophical interests of the epoch also directed attention toward astronomy. The works of the medieval Spanish-Jewish philosophers, which the Polish Jews were studying, abound with excursions into astronomy. The world of the stars occupied much space in the writings of the medieval philosophers, who sought to convey a comprehensive picture of the universe. The philosophical works thus introduced the reader to the world of the planets. Last, but not least, every student of the Jewish law had to have some knowledge of the planets when he came to deal with the intricacies of Jewish calendation. This was the reason why the great sages favored the study of astronomy. Rabbi Samuel Edels considered it one of the prerequisites for the study of the Torah, and Rabbi Ephraim Lunchits considered it an important step on "the ladder of knowledge."

The most important works in which Polish Jews studied astronomy were Hilkhoth Kiddush Hahodesh, the Laws of the Sanctification of the New Moon of Moses Maimonides and *Tsurath Haarets* by Abraham bar Hiya the Prince. In the *Book of Seasons*, the third part of his *Code of Laws*, Maimonides describes the matters pertaining to the announcement of the New Moon, and the Jewish calendar in general. And since he is sure, says Maimonides, that people desirous of knowledge will seek to understand the basis on which the Sanhedrin used to figure the time of the New Moon and the holidays, he offers a description of all the celestial bodies and their movements. This concise and clear presentation was easily available to the average student of the Talmud. To this chapter of Maimonides' *Code,* Rabbi Mordecai Yaffe composed a special commentary with explanatory drawings. He also wrote extensive astronomical observations in his work *Levush Hatekheleth, The Raiment of Blue Cloth,* on the occasion of discussing the laws of the New Moon. A penetrating analysis of the Jewish calendar is also found in a responsum of Rabbi Benjamin Solnik which is included in his work *Maseath Binyamin.*

While the preoccupation with the problems of Jewish calendation induced Polish-Jewish scholars to study the astronomical writings of Maimonides, their interest in the book *Tsurath*

Haarets was purely theoretical. This work by Abraham bar Hiya Hanasi, who lived in Barcelona in the first half of the twelfth century, is the oldest astronomical work written in the Hebrew language. Testimony to the great interest of Poland's Jewish scholars in this work are Rabbi Moses Isserles' many quotes from it in his writings, and Mordecai Yaffe's, Matathiah Delakrut's, and Manoah Hendel's formal commentaries on it.

Maimonides' Laws on the New Moon and the work *Tsurath Haarets* turned out to be good textbooks, and the knowledge of astronomy was quite widespread among Polish Jewry. True, Rabbi Moses Isserles and Rabbi Ephraim Lunchits believed in the geocentric theories long after Nicholas Copernicus had died (1543). Nevertheless, the Polish-Jewish scholars felt at home in the science of astronomy. This is evident from their frequent criticisms of the astronomical errors of preceding generations. Rabbi Mordecai Yaffe blamed the erroneous explanation of the rules of the Friday night services by a fifteenth-century German Talmudist on his ignorance of astronomy. He then gave a correct presentation of the rules on the basis of what he had learned from the "divine astronomers."

Moses Isserles went much further. After stating in the manner of the humanists that no errors could be found in the writings of the Rabbis, he goes on to say that one nevertheless gets the initial impression that contradictions do exist between them and the scientists who study the universe, especially the astronomers. He then criticizes quite openly the opinion of Rabbi Joshua regarding the position of the sun in the sky (Baba Bathra 25 b) by stating that this opinion is "far from being reasonable." Talmudic scholars who had the courage to criticize Tannaitic opinions in this manner surely were self-confident about their expertise in astronomy.

Polish-Jewish scholars also took an interest in the work *Theorica Planetarum* of the astronomer George Purbach who lived in Vienna and in Cracow in the fifteenth century. Interest in this work was great in Poland, probably because it was written while its author lived in Cracow. A Hebrew translation of *Theorica Planetarum* is known under the name *Mahalakh*

Hakokhavim, The Movement of the Planets. Moses Isserles was profoundly interested in this work. He quoted it in *Torath Haolah* and wrote an explanatory commentary on it. Before Isserles, Matathiah Delakrut studied Purbach's work and quoted it frequently in one of his books. Delakrut is possibly the author of another commentary on *Theorica Planetarum* which is preserved only in manuscript. We also have a very beautiful commentary on this widely read astronomical work from the pen of the polyhistor Manoah Hendel. It may be worthwhile mentioning that in the 17th century a Polish-Jewish scholar wrote Addenda to Isserles' commentary on *Theorica Planetarum.*

Matathiah Delakrut is also the author of additional works on astronomy. He wrote a commentary on the book *Mareh Haofanim, The Image of the Spheres,* which is a Hebrew translation of the much-read short treatise on astronomy *Sphaera Mundi* by the 13th century scholar Johannes de Sacrobosco. Matathiah painstakingly wrote his commentary and compared the Hebrew translation with the Latin original. Additional notes by Manoah Hendel found their way into Matathiah's commentary. Matathiah's best-known work is the already mentioned *Tsel Haolam, Image of the World.* This is a treatise on cosmography which, as we have seen, is a rearrangement of the French work *Image du monde,* written in the 13th century. Matathiah divides the description of the universe into three parts. The first part describes man and the globe. The second part is a geography of the continents and a description of the various climates. The third part contains a somewhat strange compilation of facts about astronomy, philosophy, and . . . paradise. As mentioned above, Matathiah composed this work to fill the gap in scientific knowledge that existed between Jews and Gentiles. A hundred years after the author's death, the book was printed several times.

Information supplied by Rabbi Manoah Hendel shows us that in the area of astronomy he was the most prolific writer among the Polish Jews. He wrote commentaries on five well-known astronomical works. Moreover, he was the author of the only original work in astronomy produced by Polish Jewry in that epoch: *Astronomic Charts* "in which one can find exact information on the location of the various stars . . . and all that happens to them . . . at any time and in each hour." We may add, however, that these works were never printed. Unknown also is the book of astronomy authored by Joshua Falk, according to a statement of his son.

It may be said in conclusion that Moses Isserles' enthusiastic preoccupation with astronomy made a significant impact on his pupil, David Gans of Prague. To his influence we may ascribe David's decision to write the work *Nehemad Wenaim, The Desirable and the Delightful,* a reference book on astronomy which also discusses the laws regarding the proclamation of the New Moon.

VII.

The science of medicine was, of course, the only discipline which did not evoke any opposition. Curiously, however, very little, if anything, was contributed by Polish Jewry of that period in this area of knowledge. It was significantly inferior to Polish Jewry's contribution to astronomy or even to mathematics. It should be emphasized at this point that sixteenth-century Poland contributed rather little in the area of medical research, although the country had many illustrious doctors and large collections of medical works.

Jewish doctors were known in Poland as early as the fifteenth century. Ignacy Schipper has compiled a list of about twenty Jewish doctors who practiced between 1435 and 1527. There is no doubt that the actual number of Jewish physicians was much larger. Whenever historical research is conducted on the local level, names of Jewish doctors are usually discovered. About the year 1500 we find Jewish doctors in Cracow, Warsaw, and also in the vicinity of Posen. It is worth noting that there was a woman doctor among them. It is difficult to ascertain whether these were physicians trained in universities or medical practitioners who acquired their knowledge through apprenticeship. It is generally agreed that most of these doctors were not graduates of medical schools. Among fifteen Jewish doctors who lived in the region of Posen during the sixteenth century, only two had professional diplomas.

The only university at which Polish Jews were permitted to matriculate as students of medicine was that of Padua in Italy. The Polish "nation" among the students of Padua was generally very large. Gentile students from Poland frequently studied also at various German universities. Jews however, were barred from enrollment in German schools. The earliest information about Polish-Jewish students in Padua is from the year 1501. Their number grew steadily all through the sixteenth century and became especially large after 1650. Interestingly enough, some Polish magnates awarded stipends to young Jews to enable them to study medicine in Padua.

Besides the native Jewish doctors, there was also a number of immigrant Jewish physicians in Poland. At the time of the expulsion of 1492, a number of well-trained Spanish-Jewish physicians settled in Poland. Very prominent among them became the Calahora family. Learned Jewish physicians also arrived from Italy. When the Polish queen Bona, an Italian princess, came to Cracow in 1518, she brought along a few Jewish physicians from her homeland. All these physicians were in great demand, and practiced mainly at the royal court and among the high nobility. One of the Spanish-Jewish physicians, Isaac, was held in especially high esteem and was given many privileges and precious gifts both by the royal family and the hierarchy. When a certain Lithuanian doctor met an eminent Jewish physician at the court of Duke Albrecht of nearby Prussia, he immediately persuaded him to leave and settle in Vilna. Here and there Jewish doctors were even appointed by municipalities as public health officers.

The Jewish religious leaders manifested a very friendly attitude to the medical profession. In the sixteenth century, a general awareness of the need for medical care arose in Eastern Europe. This, of course, greatly enhanced the social status of the physicians. Rabbi Meir of Lublin addressed a doctor as "the scholar perfect in all areas of knowledge and wise in counsel." Rabbi Mordecai Yaffe explicitly permitted the Jewish physicians to dress in the garb worn by their Gentile colleagues, at a time when ordinary Jews were expected to don characteristically Jewish clothes. The eminent author, Moses the Dead, discussed the personality of the Jewish doctor in forceful statements. He recommended that no one should rely on nature's cure, but should always seek the aid of a physician and the use of medications. "But no man," he warns, "should practice the art of medicine who is not expertly trained in this field, . . . as many are the victims of untrained medics." He approves of the high fees paid to physicians, "as the doctor is paid for his knowledge, and the price of knowledge has no limits." He demands, however, that physicians should not be paid for training their apprentices. Rabbi Solomon Luria admired the art of medicine for a different reason. He believed that doctors might be able to clarify many of the intricate rules pertaining to the dietary laws.

A certain amount of practical medical knowledge could be found among the rabbis. We may assume that they acquired their information in the many works of medieval Hebrew medical literature. The writings of Rabbi Mordecai Yaffe offer a number of dietetic instructions. Ephraim Lunchits also gives dietetic advice "in a way recommended by the physicians." We also find other medical observations in his writings. A considerable quantity of advice is interspersed in *Matenoth Kehunah,* the commentary to Midrash Rabbah. The source of this material, says the author, are "the books of medicines." Rabbi Faivish of Cracow (died 1618) is the author of a responsum filled with information on anatomy and medicine in general. The responsum clearly implies that its author was a devoted reader of medical works.

What could be termed a medical literature *per se* did not exist among the Jews of Eastern Europe at that time. If the assumption that the pamphlet *Luah Hayim, Tablet of Life,* was written by Doctor Solomon Luria, namesake and relative of Rabbi Solomon Luria, is correct, it was the only medical work produced by Polish Jewry in that era.

VIII.

The attitude of sixteenth century Polish Jewry to the philosophical disciplines was not unequivocal. We have seen above how Rabbi Solomon Luria reproached his younger friend Moses Isserles for his and his pupil's interest in philosophy. On the other hand, he admitted that he himself was well versed in philosophical literature. The same attitude generally prevailed during the latter decades of the century. Many of the scholars were trained in philosophy, but approved of its study only under certain conditions. Some, like Moses the Dead, thought that the study of philosophy was perhaps a transgression of the Rabbis' prohibition of "Greek wisdom." Even Rabbi Moses Isserles and Rabbi Ephraim Lunchits, the two men closest to philosophy, did not think that this discipline could offer a satisfactory answer to the basic problem of the essence of God. Isserles was of the opinion that the philosophers spend many years to gain the knowledge "which an ordinary Jew may attain by studying Torah." The strongest opposition could be noticed, of course, among the Kabbalists. Rabbi Isaiah Horowitz candidly expressed their views when he attacked "the Jewish scholars who were captivated by the Greek wisdom and thus were turning the true words of the Torah into wormwood" (cf. Amos 5:7). The only noted scholar whose attitude toward philosophy was one of complete indifference, was Rabbi Meir of Lublin.

A bitter fight about the study of philosophy broke out in Posen in 1559. The chief rabbi of the community at that time was a certain Aaron, an immigrant from Prague. He was a decided opponent of philosophy and of secular studies in general. Because of this attitude, Rabbi Aaron became involved, while still in Prague, in a sharp conflict with another scholar whose name is unknown to us. By what was probably a coincidence, Rabbi Aaron's adversary also settled in Posen at the time of Rabbi Aaron's ministry to this community. In 1559 Rabbi Aaron sharply attacked philosophy in his *Shabbath Hagadol* (i.e., the Sabbath preceding Passover) sermon and even spoke of Maimonides' *Guide of the Perplexed* in a derogatory manner. Rabbi Aaron's anonymous adversary evidently could not take this attack calmly and responded with a skillfully written pamphlet. The manuscript of a part of this pamphlet has been preserved, but does not contain sufficient clues to identify the author. The hypothesis that the author was Abraham Horovitz, Isaiah's father, has no real basis. Whoever the author may have been, he was very well versed both in the Talmud and the sciences. His Hebrew style is excellent and he utilizes his linguistic skills to ridicule and belittle Rabbi Aaron in the manner of his Italian humanist colleagues. He heaps many insults upon him and, by using certain homonyms, charges that Rabbi Aaron is not in possession of a "tradition based on wisdom," but rather of a "tradition based on foolishness." The most interesting aspect of the controversy, as appears from the partial text, is the fact that neither Rabbi Aaron nor the anonymous defender of philosophy were fighting it out alone. Each was backed by a group of supporters, who either ardently loved philosophy or passionately hated it.

The anonymous admirer of philosophy asserts that Aaron was the only East European rabbi who rejected the philosophical writings of Moses Maimonides. Rabbi Aaron used the old argument that late in life Maimonides regretted having composed philosophical works. Most Polish opponents of philosophy, however, abstained from criticizing the "Great Eagle" (i.e. Maimonides) for his preoccupation with philosophy. There was, on the contrary a genuine admiration for Moses Maimonides among the Jews of the Polish Lithuanian Commonwealth. We have seen how Rabbi Moses Isserles was fascinated by Maimonides' teachings and how he mentioned the *Guide of the Perplexed* almost on every page of his work *Torath Haolah*. Indeed, according to the author of the pamphlet, "this book, *The Guide of the Perplexed,* was studied and

taught (in Poland)." Rabbi Abraham Horovitz reported, at
the same time, that during the vacation periods in the yeshivahs
much time was given to the study of Maimonides' "Eight
Chapters," which is his introduction to the Sayings of the
Fathers. In his admiration for Maimonides, the anonymous
philosopher went as far as to state that the "Great Eagle" was
capable of predicting the future like a prophet. Rabbi Mordecai Yaffe, although more cautious in his admiration of Maimonides, also fully understood the importance of *The Guide
of the Perplexed* in the realm of Jewish thought, and termed it
"the famous book of wisdom which includes all the sciences
which the philosophers studied." Similarly, it is obvious that
Rabbi Samuel Edels, whose interest in the Aggadah was deep
and genuine, was an ardent reader of the *Guide*. Rabbi Isaiah
Horovitz, the all-out kabbalist, who considered philosophy
a superfluous discipline, also had much esteem for Maimonides
the jurist, if not the philosopher.

The admiration of Polish-Jewish scholars for Moses Maimonides is further attested by the fact that a considerable part of
their literary production in philosophy was centered around
his writings. Besides quoting Maimonides hundreds of times
in *Torath Haolah,* Moses Isserles also wrote short remarks to
the *Guide*. Similar glossae to the *Guide* were written by Rabbi
Menahem ben Isaac, known as Maharam of Tykocin. A more
comprehensive, though not very profound, commentary on the
Guide was written by Rabbi Mordecai Yaffe. He included this
book, named *Pinnath Yikrath, The Costly Cornerstone* (comp.
Isaiah 28:16), in his great work, the *Levush*. Nothing is
known of the character of Manoah Hendel's commentary on the
Guide, since, like most of his works, it remained unprinted
and consequently was lost.

A wondrous work on the *Guide of the Perplexed* was composed by Joseph ben Isaac Halevi, a young, totally unknown
philosopher from Lithuania. We find him in Prague early in
the seventeenth century, where he belonged to the circle of
Rabbi Ephraim Lunchits. He instructed the then young Yomtov Lippman Heller, already a member of the Rabbinical court,

in philosophy. Joseph's work *Giveath Hamoreh* (comp. Judges 7:1), published in Prague in 1614, though full of admiration for Maimonides, critically analyzes the latter's method of thinking, as manifested in the *Guide*. In another work entitled *Kethoneth Passim, Coat of Many Colours* (an allusion to the author's name, comp. Genesis 37:3), Joseph Halevi made an attempt to prove that the Torah is superior to the Seven Liberal Arts. This work also revolves around the *Guide of the Perplexed*. Both works being very rare are little known even among scholars. *Kethoneth Passim* was printed in Lublin in 1614, and it is therefore possible that Joseph Halevi had returned to Poland the same year.

We are told by Abraham Horovitz that the interest in Maimonides' *Eight Chapters* was equally widespread. A number of commentaries on this treatise were composed in Poland during this period. The anonymous philosopher in Posen wrote such a commentary which, regrettably, is lost. Manoah Hendel's commentary on *Eight Chapters* also remained unprinted. The commentary *Hesed Avraham, Abraham's Kindness* (comp. Genesis 24:12) written by Abraham Horovitz is well known and popular. He wrote his commentary in order to enable the average man to study Maimonides' treatise without the help of an instructor. In an addendum, Abraham Horovitz presented a rather difficult commentary on Samuel ibn Tibbon's Introduction to *Eight Chapters*. The commentary *Hesed Avraham* is available in two versions. The first version was published in 1577. In the new edition, published in the beginning of the seventeenth century, the author purged his early work of much that was contained in the first version. Abraham Horovitz borrowed the material used in *Hesed Avraham* from many philosophical works, especially from the *Guide of the Perplexed* and the *Sefer Haikkarim (The Book of Principles)* by Joseph Albo, the great Spanish rabbi-philosopher of the fifteenth century.

The Book of Principles attracted the special attention of sixteenth century Polish-Lithuanian Jewry. Philosophically trained authors, such as Rabbi Ephraim Lunchits and Isaac of Troki, frequently quoted it. Rabbi Moses the Dead and Rabbi

Samuel Edels went as far as to accept Albo's three dogmas of the Unity of God, the Divine Origin of the Torah, and Reward and Punishment as the basis of the Jewish faith. Other scholars wrote formal commentaries to the work. Manoah Hendel's commentary, like most of his works, remained unprinted. But the commentary *Ohel Yaakov, Jacob's Tent* (comp. Genesis 31:33), by the above-mentioned mathematician Jacob Koppelman of Brzesc Kujawski, was printed twice, first in Germany and the second time at the end of the century in Cracow. We have seen that *Ohel Yaakov* is permeated with mathematical discussions. Being a mathematician, the author attempted to demonstrate the essence of God and the harmonious interdependence of all phenomena in the universe by mathematical proofs.

Except for the few commentaries on the *Guide of the Perplexed* and *Book of Principles,* little was written in Poland in the area of philosophy during this period. Here and there the introduction to a work in Rabbinics mentions that the author also composed philosophical writings. All those writings, however, have since been lost and nothing can be said about their possible value. Manoah Hendel's commentaries to various other medieval philosophical works also remained unknown. We find some consolation in the only work of Rabbi Manoah Hendel that was printed and saved for posterity, his commentary on Rabbi Bahya ibn Pakuda's *Hovoth Halevavoth, The Duties of the Heart,* named *Manoah Halevavoth, The Tranquility of the Heart.* There was genuine interest in Bahya's popular philosophic-ethical work in Poland at that time, although it could not compare with the great interest in the *Guide of the Perplexed* and *The Book of Principles.* Manoah Hendel tells us that his commentary grew out of discussions conducted by a study group under his guidance. The author made an effort to adjust his commentary to the needs of the average student of philosophy, and rewrote the book several times before printing it in Cracow in 1596. This beautiful commentary on *The Duties of the Heart* was later reprinted several times in Germany and in Poland.

The information presented above makes it clear that despite the paucity of local philosophical literature and the existence of an opposition, the interest in, and knowledge of, philosophy were quite widespread among the Polish Jews of the late sixteenth century. Of the about two hundred Hebrew books published at the time, ten belonged to the various philosophical disciplines. Since, however, most of the philosophical works of Spanish Jewry were very often quoted by Polish-Jewish authors, we will have to assume that many books in the area of philosophy were imported from other countries for sale in Poland. The high degree of knowledge of Jewish philosophy is further attested to by the basic familiarity of Polish-Jewish authors (the Anonymous of Posen, Moses the Dead, Isaac of Troki, David the Preacher and, of course, Rabbi Moses Isserles) with Jewish philosophical terminology. If we assume that Rabbi Moses Isserles, Rabbi Ephraim Lunchits, and most other jurists devoted only their leisure time to the study of philosophical works, this certainly was not the case with the anonymous philosopher of Posen. No doubt, Joseph Halevi or Isaac of Troki, the author of *Hizzuk Emunah,* devoted much more than their leisure time to their philosophical studies. It may be worthwhile to note that these two men, the best philosophically trained scholars, were Lithuanian Jews. It seems that Lithuania offered better opportunities for acquiring a knowledge of philosophy, either by the presence there of expert philosophers, or by the greater availability of philosophical books.

IX.

An interesting branch of Jewish literature in the Polish-Lithuanian Commonwealth were polemical works against Christianity. Judaizing tendencies appeared in the nearby Muscovite countries as early as the fifteenth century. During the sixteenth century interest in Judaism as a religion increased considerably. Various strands of the Reformation invaded Poland from the West and called the attention of the people to the Bible, and to Judaism as the mother religion of Christianity. During the second half of the century a great revival could be noticed in Polish theological literature, and some basic works in this field were written. Most of the Protestant books were written in Polish and were widely circulated. Of great importance was Simon Budny's Polish translation of the Bible with a remarkably good commentary. A number of Christians converted to Judaism, and in various towns Christian men and women were put on trial for practicing Jewish religious customs. Quite sensational was the case of Catherine Weigel, the widow of a renowned Cracow patrician, who converted to Judaism in the 1530's and was ultimately burned at the stake. When more cases of conversion to Judaism occurred, the government began to take stronger action. A Judaizing movement also arose in various Muscovite cities, such as Moscow, Kiev and Novgorod, although only few Jews lived there at the time. The Muscovite government fought these tendencies mercilessly. During the reign of Ivan the Terrible (1533–1584), seven Russian Orthodox priests fled to Lithuania, converted to Judaism and began to attack their former faith. One of them, Theodosius Kosa, developed a new radically anti-Christian doctrine known as Theodosianism. This heresy had many followers in the eastern provinces of the Polish-Lithuanian Commonwealth.

It is not yet known what part Jews played in this Judaizing ferment among the Christians. The Church accused the Jews of conducting missionary activities among the Christians. They allegedly clandestinely converted many Christians to Judaism and sent them to the Balkan countries, then under Turkish domination. At the time of the Catherine Weigel trial, the cantor of a Cracow synagogue was compelled to flee to Turkey and the rabbis and the lay leaders of the community were arrested. The persecutions of the Jews of Lithuania, the center of the Judaizing movement, were so severe that they plunged the country into a serious economic depression. Although religious disputations were fraught with danger, Polish Jews did not evade them altogether. In the court of King Casimir Jagiellonczyk (1447–1492) religious disputations were often conducted with the participation of a Jew. The chronicler Dietz tells us that a certain Jew was interrogated by an inquisitor in a Cracow church; the Jew courageously defended himself and was ultimately burned at the stake. At a later date, we find Jewish scholars interested in the famous anti-Christian polemical work *Sefer Nizzahon,* whose author Yomtov Lippmann Muehlhausen, as we have seen, possibly wrote it in Cracow more than one hundred and fifty years earlier. The work is quoted by Ephraim Lunchits and Moses the Dead. The latter parenthetically tells us that a certain Christian asked him about matters of religion.

All this information, fragmentary as it is, indicates that religious disputations between Jews and Christians occurred rather frequently in Eastern Europe. Truly interesting in this regard are two books which were published in Poland in the second half of the century and which are important contributions to religious literature. The first is a book published in Polish in 1581 and written by a certain Nahman (alias Jacob) of Belzec. The book contains a reply by Nahman to a challenge by Martin Czechowicz, one of the main figures in Poland's Reformation turmoil. Czechowicz often provoked disputations with Jews and Judaizing Christians. Out of these dialogues grew two books in which Czechowicz attacked the Jewish religion. Nahman's reply, *Odpis na Dyalogi Czechowicza, Reply to the Dialogues of Czechowicz,* contains a defense of the foundations of Judaism, as well as an admonition to the Christian party not to incite the Christian populace against the Jews during the disputations. It should be noted, however, that it was the opinion of Majer Balaban, one of the most knowledgeable students of the Jewish past in Poland, that "Nahman of Belzec" is a pseudonym behind which Czechowicz himself hid. According to Balaban, Czechowicz wrote this treatise to give himself an opportunity to rebut the arguments advanced by Jews in the religious disputations.

The second book, *Hizzuk Emunah, Strengthening of the Faith,* is one of the best polemical works ever written on the

Jewish side. The personality of the author, Isaac ben Abraham of Troki (a town in the vicinity of Vilna) has long been a subject of discussion among scholars. When the book first became known at the end of the seventeenth century, nobody thought that the author was a Karaite. He often quotes passages from the Talmud and is generally quite similar to other Jewish authors. It is, however, strange that an author as brilliant as Isaac ben Abraham was never mentioned by hundreds of Jewish authors throughout the seventeenth and eighteenth centuries. It should also be noted, that although the author quotes many passages from the Talmud, he never says a word in defense of this great and often-attacked work of the Jewish mind. Several years after *Hizzuk Emunah* was first published, a Karaite writer listed Isaac ben Abraham as one of the important Karaite authors. He also stated that Isaac of Troki was his great grandfather's brother. This, together with the facts mentioned above are the basis for the assumption that the author of *Hizzuk Emunah* was a Karaite. Many a Karaite author, like Isaac, quoted passages from the Talmud.

The problem of Isaac's religious affiliation has still not been settled. Majer Balaban, who did important research in the history of Poland's Karaites, is of the opinion that Isaac of Troki was, indeed, a Karaite. He argues that during the century which elapsed between the composition of the work and its first printing, Rabbinic authors interpolated it with "Rabbanite" material, thus depriving it of its distinctive Karaitic character. The same historian contends that the book could not have been published at the time of its composition because Poland was then already ruled by Sigismund III (1588–1632), and the Catholic reaction was firmly in its saddle. Taking all the above facts into consideration, we tend to believe that *Hizzuk Emunah* was originally written by a Karaite. In its present form, however, the book was rewritten by a Rabbanite Jew who probably changed it greatly by omitting parts of the original text and replacing them with new material.

Despite the rewriting that *Hizzuk Emunah* may have undergone, it is in many respects an excellent polemical work. The author was a highly educated man, a kind of polyhistor, and his work is a religio-philosophical treatise of great depth. The author had a critical mind and easily discovered contradictions in the New Testament. In addition, he wrote his work after having conducted a long series of religious debates with members of the nobility, the clergy, and the judiciary. He thus was properly prepared for his task. The material in the book is well organized. In the one hundred chapters into which the two parts of the book are divided, we first find a refutation of the accusations that Christians made against the Jews. This is followed by arguments against Christianity and by a list of contradictions that can be found in the New Testament. The book was repeatedly printed in the Hebrew original and was translated into nearly all modern languages. Eighteenth century opponents of religion, including Voltaire, borrowed material from *Hizzuk Emunah* for their attacks on the Church and its dogmas. This work, composed at the end of the sixteenth century, may be considered the conclusion of the humanist epoch, in which Polish-Lithuanian Jewry clung to Talmudic research, but also maintained contact with the various currents of general culture.

X.

Polish-Lithuanian Jewry was also quite interested in the Jewish past. But in this area, too, it stopped short of any significant achievement. During this golden epoch of Jewish historiography, when Italian Jewry produced almost all the major Jewish chronicles and Azariah dei Rossi wrote his magnificent critical work *Meor Enayim, The Light of the Eyes* (comp. Proverbs 15:30), Polish Jewry produced only fragmentary contributions of limited significance.

That there existed an interest in the past can be seen from the fact that the Hebrew printing press in Cracow during this period published no less than ten historical books, including such important chronicles as *Yosippon, Sefer Yohasin,* and

Shalsheleth Hakabbalah. Several books of the Apocrypha and the tales about the destruction of Jerusalem found in the Talmud were published as well. There is also significance in the fact that some of these books were published in Yiddish, such as *Shevet Yehudah* and *Die Wiener Gezerah,* which describes the destruction of Austrian Jewry in the years 1420–1421.

The interest in history is further demonstrated by Moses Isserles' already mentioned liberal approach to the question of whether it is permissible to read historical books on the Sabbath. The *Shulhan Arukh* (Orah Hayim, chapter 307, paragraph 16) prohibits the reading of non-religious literature on the Sabbath in general. Isserles added the statement that "secular literature and stories of wars" may be read on the Sabbath if they are written in the holy tongue. "Stories of wars" presumably refers to historical literature. Isserles' pupil David Gans quotes this opinion of his teacher in the introduction to the second part of his chronicle *Tsemah David, Shoot of David,* (comp. Jeremiah 23:5), in order to demonstrate the permissibility of reading historical literature.

The history books that appeared in print in Poland, and the dispensation given by Rabbi Moses Isserles, indicate that the reading of history was quite widespread. Isserles' permit to read historical literature in Hebrew further shows that a longing for this kind of literature existed among that portion of the intelligentsia which was capable of reading Hebrew. Historical information widely scattered in the writings of the Polish-Jewish authors indicates that they acquired a knowledge of the past from sources such as *Yossipon* and other medieval historical works. Rabbi Solomon Luria possessed a certain amount of knowledge of general history. Isaac of Troki surpassed him by far in this respect. Isaac seems to have carefully read Martin Bielski's *Kronika Swiata Wszystkiego, A Chronicle of All the World,* which was a popular historical work written in the vernacular and published in 1556. Isaac's knowledge of foreign countries and their constitutional structures was quite remarkable.

Against this backdrop, Polish Jewry's literary production in the area of historiography appears to have been extremely poor.

Sixteenth century Polish historiography was in general inferior by far to that of the preceding century. But still a number of important works were composed even in the sixteenth century, such as the above-mentioned world chronicle by Martin Bielski, the historical writings of Martin Kromer, and many other historical and biographical works. By comparison, Polish Jewry's historical literature, if it may be so called, was meager. Most important, no doubt, is Moses Isserles' deep interest in history. In his philosophical work *Torath Haolah* he wrote so extensively about the Temple in Jerusalem and the sacrificial service that, even though this may not have been his intention, he added an important chapter to Jewish archaeology. He also wrote addenda to a chapter dealing with chronology in Isaac Israeli's work on geometry and astronomy, *Yesod Olam, Foundation of the World*. This chapter, corrected by Moses Isserles, together with additional information that he collected about the chronology of the sages from Rashi to Rabbi Shakhna, was from 1581 onwards almost regularly reprinted in the various editions of *Sefer Yohasin,* the famous chronicle of Abraham Zacuto. Isserles had prepared this material for himself because Jewish jurists had to know, at least in part, the chronology of the sages of all times. We see, thus, that Moses Isserles' interest in the past directed itself primarily to the area of literary history. Similar short writings in the area of literary history are also encountered in the works of other 16th century Polish authors, mainly in the introductions to their books. The writings of Rabbi Solomon Luria and Rabbi Mordecai Yaffe are good examples. They used the Introduction to Maimonides' *Mishneh Torah* as a model for their treatises. The most original student of the chronology of the sages was Solomon Luria. In a responsum addressed to an interested group of people who wanted to know the "order of relationship between the great scholars, authors of books," he was able to give quite detailed information about Jewish scholarly work in France, Germany, and Italy. He gathered most of this information from the vast Rabbinic literature in which he was at home, and some from fragmentary historical writings of preceding eras. This responsum (par. 29) became a widely used source in modern Jewish historiography. But with this responsum, sixteenth-century Eastern European Jewry's contribution to Jewish historiography was concluded.

Knowledge of geography among Polish-Jewish scholars was also of a sporadic nature. A geographical literature was all but non-existent. About the only thing in this area is that part of *The Image of the World,* translated by Matathiah Delakrut, which contains much information on India and its curiosities, and very little about Europe and Africa. Geographic information in Polish-Jewish literature of the period is thus very scarce, and wherever it is found, it is mostly erroneous.

The sole exception is again the author of *Hizzuk Emunah,* who explicitly tells us that he borrowed his geographical information from "stories printed in Christian books." Of a wider scope was the understanding that Polish-Jewish scholars had of the political, legal, and economic conditions of their country and of other countries. Moses Isserles, Eliezer Ashkenazi, and to an even greater degree Ephraim Lunchits had a deep understanding of political science. Here, too, however, Isaak of Troki was best educated. He possessed detailed information about the Turkish empire, for example, and about the wars between Catholics and Protestants in Western Europe. His knowledge of the constitutional diversities of the various nations was excellent.

Polish-Jewish scholars were deeply interested in economics. To be sure, they probably did not study specialized economic literature. But they were jurists and on numerous occasions had to analyze economic problems from the point of view of the *halakhah,* both theoretically and as judges in cases of civil law. They thus acquired a thorough knowledge of the economic forces and of the new economic problems which were then emerging. Solomon Luria, Mordecai Yaffe, and later Samuel Edels, among others, often manifested their knowledge of such matters as export, import, and credit. Their remarks were so numerous that, if collected, enough material would have existed for formal treatises on various aspects of economic life.

More than they, however, the great moralist-preacher Rabbi Ephraim Lunchits was preoccupied with problems of the economic life. His interest went far beyond the legal problems, as he was deeply intrigued by the moral and social aspects of economic life. What was to his contemporaries only another issue to be dealt with from the halakhic point of view, became all important to him. For a considerable span of time, he was the only true student of the social and economic life of Polish Jewry.

CHAPTER SEVEN

EPILOGUE

In the early seventeenth century, dark clouds began to roll over Poland. The country's political structure quivered; the power of the central government weakened; a creeping anarchy spread throughout the country. The Ukrainian Cossacks who inhabited the prairies of the southeastern parts of the Commonwealth became agitated. The outbreak of a dangerous uprising under Bohdan Chmielnicki became imminent.

Under these circumstances the economy declined. The general prosperity of the sixteenth century came to an end.

Against this backdrop, the situation of Poland's Jewry took a definite turn for the worse. The increasing influence which the Catholic Church and the Jesuits had over king Sigismund III Vasa created an atmosphere of intolerance toward non-conformist groups. The Jews were, of course, among the main victims of this new bigotry.

These new conditions greatly influenced the cultural life of Poland's Jewry. The Talmudic academies still pulsated with energetic activities. The young still aspired to become scholars. In the seventeenth century the four main commentaries on the *Shulhan Arukh* were produced in Poland. Students still utilize these commentaries today. In the middle of the century, Nathan Hanover could still write that ". . . Nowhere throughout the Dispersions of Israel was there so much learning as in the Kingdom of Poland."

A definite decline was nonetheless noticeable in the cultural life of the Jewish community. The very fact that Poland's Jewish scholars were mainly bent on composing commentaries

174

on the *Shulhan Arukh* clearly indicates that the humanistic spirit of free research in the Talmud was waning.

Simultaneously, a phenomenon hitherto unknown began to appear—a surplus of scholars. The individual Jew, as well as his communal institutions, was no longer able to supply decent living conditions to young men who aspired to make the study of Talmud their career. Consequently, scholars and men belonging to the professional intelligentsia were among the first to emigrate to Western countries, where the rising new Jewish communities could absorb them and where they found many opportunities in the fields for which they were trained in Polish yeshivahs. All through the seventeenth and eighteenth centuries an uninterrupted stream of intellectuals from Poland poured into the countries of the West.

During the more than one hundred years between the conclusion of the Cossack uprisings and the partitions of the old Polish Commonwealth during the last decades of the eighteenth century, Poland's Jewry made heroic efforts to live up to its tradition of being the greatest center for the study of Torah. Although the cultural achievements of these one hundred years could by no means be compared to the immense intellectual harvest of the classical epoch, they nonetheless became the breeding ground for a new colossal expansion of Jewish religious experience and learning. Before Poland's Jewry was transformed into the three separate communities of Russian Jewry, Galician Jewry, and Prussian Jewry, it produced two of its greatest sons, Israel Baal Shem Tov ("Master of the Good Name") and the Gaon of Vilna. In a tiny town in the southeastern corner of the Commonwealth, Rabbi Israel began to teach ideas which coalesced into Hasidism, one of mankind's profoundest religious innovations. At about the same time, Rabbi Elijah, in the northeastern city of Vilna, who spent most of his life in his private study, inspired a small group of fellow students to a renewed intellectual zeal which launched a remarkable new era of Jewish scholarship in nineteenth century Lithuania.

The classical epoch of Jewish culture in Poland is linked with golden strands to earlier great centers of Jewish culture in Babylon, medieval Ashkenaz, and Spain. Similar ties also exist between the classical period and the intellectual accomplishments of later times. As one looks back now at this classical epoch, with its intellectual struggles and cultural achievements, one can only echo Nathan Hanover's assertion that nowhere indeed was there so much learning as in the Kingdom of Poland.

INDEX